THE ARCHAEOLOGY OF PERSONHOOD

Understanding personhood, the notion of what it means to be a person, can reveal a great deal about societies in any place in any time. It is therefore highly relevant to those reconstructing past social worlds from the archaeological record.

The Archaeology of Personhood examines the characteristics that define a person as a category of being, highlights how definitions of personhood are culturally variable and explores how that variation is connected to human uses of material culture. Applying an anthropological approach to detailed case studies from European prehistoric archaeology, the book explores the connection between people, animals, objects and their societies and environments; it also investigates the relationships that jointly produce bodies, persons, communities and artefacts.

Bringing together a wealth of research in social and cultural anthropology, philosophy and related fields, this is the first book to address the contribution that an understanding of personhood can make to our interpretations of the past.

Chris Fowler lectures at the University of Manchester. He is a specialist in the British Neolithic and archaeological theory, particularly focusing on concepts of the person and approaches to identity in the past.

THEMES IN ARCHAEOLOGY
Edited by Julian Thomas
University of Manchester

THE ARCHAEOLOGY OF PERSONHOOD
An anthropological approach
Chris Fowler

ARCHAEOLOGY, RITUAL, RELIGION
Timothy Insoll

THE ARCHAEOLOGY OF PERSONHOOD

An anthropological approach

Chris Fowler

Routledge
Taylor & Francis Group

LONDON AND NEW YORK

First published 2004
by Routledge
2 Park Square, Milton Park, Abingdon, Oxon, OX14 4RN

Simultaneously published in the USA and Canada
by Routledge
270 Madison Ave, New York NY 10016

RoutledgeFalmer is an imprint of the Taylor & Francis Group

Transferred to Digital Printing 2006

© 2004 Chris Fowler

Typeset in Garamond by BC Typesetting Ltd, Bristol

British Library Cataloguing in Publication Data
A catalogue record for this book is available from the British Library

Library of Congress Cataloging in Publication Data
A catalog record for this book has been requested

ISBN 0–415–31721–5 (hbk)
ISBN 0–415–31722–3 (pbk)

Publisher's Note
The publisher has gone to great lengths to ensure the quality of this reprint
but points out that some imperfections in the original may be apparent

Printed and bound by CPI Antony Rowe, Eastbourne

CONTENTS

ILLUSTRATIONS

Figures

Tables

PREFACE AND
ACKNOWLEDGEMENTS

This book first came to mind during my postgraduate research into the British and particularly Manx Neolithic. As I wrestled with the interpretation of personhood in the past I wondered why there were no books on the subject for archaeologists by archaeologists. Since then a few books have been published that address personhood, but in the main these are detailed contextual monographs, and do not introduce the anthropological approaches in great depth. The primary aim of this book is to provide a guide through interpretations of personhood for archaeologists, and to review ways that these approaches enrich the archaeological imagination. In particular the book considers recent studies of personhood within European prehistory, and the ongoing role of anthropological theories in this field. I have therefore explored the anthropological literature from an archaeologist's point of view and for archaeological purposes.

During 2000–2 I conducted research on southern Scandinavian Mesolithic and Neolithic archaeology alongside the British Neolithic, while I continued investigating theoretical approaches to personhood. This book springs from the majority of that research, although readers will not find detailed interpretations of the Neolithic material here. This research was carried out at the University of Manchester as part of a Special Research Fellowship awarded by the Leverhulme Trust. I would like to gratefully acknowledge the assistance of the Trust, and the support of the School of Art History and Archaeology at Manchester. I have benefited enormously from the expertise of my colleagues at Manchester in researching and preparing this text. Ina Berg, Vicki Cummings, Tim Insoll, Siân Jones and Julian Thomas have all read draft material and offered comments. Julian Thomas deserves special mention for all his interest in this work over the years and his continued willingness to provide advice and discuss ideas. Sarah Henson and Anne Pangbourne helped with proof-reading, and Vicki Cummings gave vital advice during preparation of the illustrations. There are a number of other people with whom I have discussed this work and who have made useful suggestions, but in particular I would like to thank Eleanor Casella, Sarah Green, Lesley MacFadyen and Rob Schmidt. The experience of teaching some very keen students interested in personhood and identity over the last two years at Manchester has been enormously beneficial in deciding how to write this book. I am also indebted to two anonymous reviewers for their comments on the draft proposal. I would like to thank Lars Larsson for permission to reprint his photograph of grave XXI at Skateholm II. I am also grateful to Chicago University Press for granting permission to reprint figure 9 from Battaglia (1990) as figure 3.1.

On a more personal note, I would like to thank Debbie, John, and Margaret Fowler, Ben, John, Liz and Sarah Henson for all their support. My family, Sarah, and her family have all endured the writing process and participated in discussions on many of the subjects covered here over the last few years. I would like to dedicate this book to the Fowlers, Hensons and Hiltons.

INTRODUCTION

Most of us wonder from time to time what people were like in the past. For example, Figure 0.1 shows the grave of three people buried together around 7,000 years ago in Denmark. How should we interpret this deposit, the bodies, objects and animal remains that it includes? What should we make of the people who were buried here, those who buried them, and the act of burial itself? How should we attempt to trace the relationships that featured in their lives, the routines of activity that shaped their experiences and bodies, the way they related to animals, places, things, and the dead? How can we tell what other people in their community were like? What strategies did they pursue in their interactions with others? In answering these questions I will argue that it is necessary to first interrogate some of our common-sense understandings of what it means to be a person, loosen their grip on our imaginations, and then illuminate some other conceptions of personhood. The reward of this approach is a far richer picture of what past people were like. While I will use only examples drawn from current research on European prehistory, both the topic of personhood and the approach presented here have a wider relevance for archaeology as a whole.

Bodies, persons and the modern world

Individuality is extremely important to us. In recent years individual lifestyle choices and experiences have become an expression

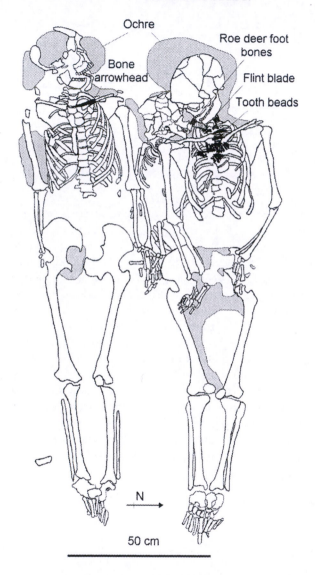

Figure 0.1 Vedbaek Bøgebakken, grave 19.

Source: Adapted from Albrethsen and Brinch Petersen (1976).

of our individuality (Giddens 1990, 1991). While we may change our lifestyles we record our personal histories in a cumulative way, building up valued biographies of remembered events and experiences. These biographies are selective and partial, though we present them as indicative of our individuality as a whole. The body is central to this project, and people continually reflect on their bodily appearance, movements and health (Shilling 1993). There is nothing new in this, but what is specifically modern is the way that these routines are carried out, the kinds of personhood they produce, and how choices are made. Each of our bodies is understood as our own property, our own project, our own business. Personal concerns are understood as private concerns centring around the knowledgeable actions of each individual. It is tempting to pursue these features in past people, to trace their individuality, the projection of their internal selves into the social world, including through their presentation of their appearance. However, this conception of individuals and individuality is emergent from the modern era, and is the result of a lengthy history, traced in the first chapter. Many prehistoric communities did not live through this history, through a world of mass production, capitalism, internalized reflection, privatized concerns, and social technologies that individuated each person and alienated people from both the wider community and nature. People in past societies were not necessarily individualized in the same way as those of modern people, and past identities may have been temporary, contextual, and community concerns. I argue here that past concepts of personhood may have supported identities that were highly contextual, and relational to specific events and interactions. In this book interpretations of contemporary ethnographies investigating personhood are used as a starting point to illuminate features such as these that are overlooked or absent in western society, and which are frequently overlooked in interpreting the past. It will be demonstrated that there are other conceptions of personhood that complement or countermand individuality, and each of which, taken as a whole, is rather unlike modern and post-modern notions of the individual. While we can reasonably assume that all people in the past were self-aware, this book aims to explore the diverse kinds of self they were aware of.

Peopling the past

It is only relatively recently that archaeologists have made concerted efforts to people the past, and to provide a humanized view of prehistory. Culture-historic approaches, dominant worldwide until the 1960s, were not concerned with individuals but with cultures, ethnic groups or even races (Jones 1997: ch. 2). Processual archaeologies generally pursued universal laws of human culture, and in so doing sought frameworks to quantify and compare social identities and statuses. Analyses of mortuary practices (e.g. Saxe 1970; Tainter 1978) drew extensively on sociological ideas about social personae and social roles drawn from sociology and sociological anthropology (e.g. Goodenough 1969). Social identities were roles people held (shaman, priest, mother), while social personae were the presentation of any combination of these roles in a specific interaction. Individuality, equated with a very personal and unique self-identity that was consistent at the core of a person (cf. Cohen 1994), was therefore kept separate from social interaction and social personae, and explicable only as a factor of innate individual preferences and psychological character traits. This understanding of people – as primarily individuals who enter into social roles – dates from liberal philosophies of the eighteenth century. In *Missing Persons*, Douglas and Ney (1998) illustrate how these ideas presume individual desires as fundamental to human nature, and society as a 'place' where these individual wills battle for survival. Aside from presenting an impoverished view of society, Douglas and Ney argue that this restrictive view of persons is dehumanizing, and fails to recognize the crucial role of contextual identities in forming the very motivations that people have. Archaeologies of personhood therefore need to attend to the cultural motivations that guide people, and people's strategies for negotiating those motivations, as well as the identities that are produced by social interaction.

In many ways, the movement to people the past is synonymous with the broad agenda of post-processual archaeology. From the late 1970s archaeologists increasingly accentuated human bodies as 'sites' for culturally specific forms of political negotiation and social disputes (e.g. Thomas 1991; Yates 1993). It was argued that people were generated through their entanglement in social, political and symbolic interactions. Renewed emphasis was placed on contextual social relationships, and in particular the negotiation of power relations and identities through the manipulation of material culture (e.g. Shanks and Tilley 1982; Shennan 1982). During this period post-processual archaeologists were inspired by work from feminist and Marxist approaches to society, and embraced new trends in anthropology and sociology, including the emerging fields of cultural studies and material culture studies (e.g. Barrett 1994; Gero and Conkey 1991; Hebdige 1979; Hodder 1982, 1986; Miller 1987; Shanks and Tilley 1987a, 1987b; Tilley 1990). Analysis shifted from finding laws that applied universally to culture, to understanding culture as something that is socially manipulated and consumed in heterogeneous ways. The emphasis on the consumer, the reader, the interpreter, shifted the focus towards heterogeneous social subgroups and even the individual person. One result of this process has been to lodge modern individuals in the 'archaeological imagination' (Thomas 1996: 63–4). This has prioritized western concepts of the person at the cost of a wide range of other ways to understand what it means to be a person. This book reviews ways that archaeologists can and have addressed that imbalance.

Personhood beyond the individual

This book examines how people emerge from an ongoing field of social relations involving humans, animals, things and places. Detailed readings in ethnographic analyses of personhood form the basis of this book since these ethnographies have also been extremely influential in the archaeological imagination, but key details are seldom explicitly explained in archaeological literature. Personhood itself is defined, along with some of the other key terms used in this book, in Box 0.1. Different societies have different concepts of the person, different understandings of the boundaries of and interpenetrations between people and things, and one person and another. Some artefacts might be features of a person, or persons in their own right. Animals and objects and even natural phenomena may be persons: not just *like* people, but actually persons in their own right sharing the same social and technological world. Archaeologies of personhood investigate how past people were generated alongside their social worlds, through social technologies, and look for the key metaphors and principles that structured daily lives. This book therefore focuses on the different social practices through which people are constituted in each context. The redistribution and circulation of bodily and worldly substances are all discussed as major features in the attainment and maintenance of personhood, where the person is one social being embedded in a larger cosmos. Special emphasis is given to the interactive production of personhood within a community, and the differing strategies people employ in negotiating their own personal identities through the larger trends in practice that structure their lives. Age, caste and gender all play a role in formulating these strategies, as these are all inseparable from personhood. While I do not attempt an exhaustive review of archaeological interpretations of personhood within European prehistory in this short book, several recent approaches are discussed. The aim of the book is not to offer critiques, but to illustrate the broad potential of these approaches and locate them within the theoretical debate over personhood in the past and present.

Box 0.1 Key definitions

Person is used to refer to any entity, human or otherwise, which may be conceptualized and treated as a person. A person is frequently composed through the temporary association of different aspects. These aspects may include features like mind, spirit or soul as well as a physical body, and denote the entity as having a form of agency. Exactly who or what may or may not be a person is contextually variable.

Personhood in its broadest definition refers to the condition or state of being a person, as it is understood in any specific context. Persons are constituted, de-constituted, maintained and altered in social practices through life and after death. This process can be described as the ongoing attainment of personhood. Personhood is frequently understood as a condition that involves constant change, and key transformations to the person occur throughout life and death. People may pass from one state or stage of personhood to another. Personhood is attained and maintained through relationships not only with other human beings but with things, places, animals and the spiritual features of the cosmos. Some of these may also emerge as persons through this engagement. People's own social interpretations of personhood and of the social practices through which personhood is realized shape their interactions in a reflexive way, but personhood remains a mutually constituted condition.

Modes of personhood, or *fields of personhood*, are terms used here to describe the overarching logic of being a person within any social context and the specific long-term trends in the practices that support that logic. Modes of personhood provide the forms that relationships are supposed to take. People

continued on next page

actively engage with these trends, and with that particular concept of personhood, when they pursue strategies of interaction. As a result of these interactions, each person is constituted in a specific way.

The following are key features of contemporary modes of personhood:

1 *Individuality and indivisibility.* Individuality in our common conception of personal uniqueness is a feature of all persons. I use the term 'indivisibility' to refer to the state of being a unitary, totalized and indivisible person. Indivisibility is a predominant trend in our contemporary western mode of personhood, and individuality lies at the core of a constant, fixed self.

2 *Individuals.* Obviously, all people are individuals in the common use of the term. I use the term 'western individual' to refer to personhood in which a constant individuality and a persistent personal identity are stressed over relational identities. All people have individuality, but the shape that it takes, the desires that characterize it, and the value accorded to it vary immensely.

3 *Dividuals and dividuality.* A state of being in which the person is recognized as composite and multiply-authored. People are composed of social relations with others to the degree that they owe parts of themselves to others. Furthermore, the person is comprised of multiple features with different origins, like a mind, soul and body, and some of these may not be fixed in the matter of the body but either enter into or emerge from the person during certain occasions. The body itself also has different constituent elements, and changes in the balance of these may alter the disposition of the person. Interactions reach into and affect the constitution of the person. All of the elements of the cosmos may pass through dividual people. Two examples of dividual personhood are discussed in detail:

continued on facing page

8

- *Partibility*. A state of being in which the dividual person is reconfigured so that one part can be extracted and given to another person to whom it is owed. Parts of oneself originate in and belong to others. These can be identified as objects and extracted. Partibility exists in tandem with dividuality, and is a key feature of personhood in many Melanesian contexts.
- *Permeable people and permeability*. A state of being in which the person is dividual, and can be permeated by qualities that influence the internal composition of the person. The component parts of the person are not identifiable as objects but as flow of substances. Permeability is a key feature of personhood in many Indian contexts.

All of these modes of personhood are constructs, but at present indivisible individuals have the greatest rein on the archaeological imagination. Relational personhood is given shape by being involved in the world in certain ways: engaging in a specific task, or acquiring a certain perspective through an event. The relationship provides the grounds in which the person takes a temporary shape. Personhood here is contextual and shifting.

These definitions will be revised, embellished and replaced throughout this book as relationships between personhood and context become more apparent, and spring from my interpretation of the debate over personhood. I have used the terms 'persons' and 'people' interchangeably for the sake of producing a more readable text. Anthropological texts do not usually do so.

The structure of this book

Chapter 1 traces a brief history of the western notion of the individual, and suggests that people in Europe did not always think of themselves as they do now. Chapter 2 examines ethnographic studies of personhood in Melanesia and India, evaluating the idea that people can be not only individual but also permeable or partible. Personhood will be compared with ethnicity, caste, age and gender to illustrate how these intersect with one another in formulating identities. Chapter 3 gives centre stage to the roles played by transactions and material exchanges in modes of personhood. It also considers how personhood might be studied through examining transformations in past material culture. Chapter 4 develops on the temporary and shifting nature of personhood by examining mortuary practices. Chapter 5 interprets the role of substances in the constitution of personhood, and the interconnections between human and non-human persons. It looks into trends in personhood as ways of maintaining the cosmos and forming connections through time. Finally, Chapter 6 offers a study of personhood in the southern Scandinavian later Mesolithic.

1

THE INDIVIDUAL IN THE ARCHAEOLOGICAL IMAGINATION

This chapter offers a brief history of the individual, exposing the problem with using one historically saturated conception of the person to refer to personhood throughout the past. This conception frames the person as a bounded, indivisible and self-determining social being who enters into relations with similarly bounded others. Here it is argued that such contemporary conceptions of individuals have consistently fed the archaeological imagination, but that it is time to change the diet. The second part of the chapter argues that ethnographic interpretations of personhood in non-western contexts produce constructs that can be compared to our common-sense notion of individuality.

Imagining individuals

Atlas of the individual: the body, the mind and the soul

Archaeologists frequently access personhood through the remains or depictions of past bodies. Yet the body is not all there is to a person, and if we study only the human body we miss out on other features that commonly compose a person. For example, in European philosophical and religious reasoning a person consists of a series of aspects, defined as the mind, the body and the soul. Scholars have repeatedly attempted to define these different aspects of the person and their relationships to each other. René

Descartes (1596–1650) argued that the mind and body were theoretically separable, and that the mind sets humans apart from the rest of the world; he placed 'I think therefore I am' as the fundamental statement of human being. The mind was the 'seat of reason', the soul the enduring aspect of the person with overtones of spiritual value, and the body was the material location of the mind and the soul. For Descartes, animals had bodies but were not endowed with the ability to think or feel, had no souls or minds, and were not persons. He also argued that the soul was not a part of the body but an entwined feature of the mind (Morris 1991: 11). All of the emotional and sensory faculties of the person were, he argued, matters of the body which could be separated from the soul. The soul was eternal and rational. The mind – as a faculty of the soul – possessed 'those qualities which the human being shares with God: freedom, will, consciousness' (Bordo 1987: 93). Descartes was attempting to elucidate the composition of the person, clearly viewing the person as a composite being. Some of these components permeated the person but originated elsewhere, since the soul was an eternal connection with God.

Individual, world and society: the emergence of the indivisible individual

It was Descartes's *project* to keep the mind separate from the inanimate matter of the world, including the body. His philosophy was not so much a description of commonly accepted reality as a manifesto. Bordo (1987: 99) argues that this project had been more or less achieved by the time Kant wrote his *Critique of Pure Reason* in the latter part of the eighteenth century. She also argues that Descartes's philosophy should be located within social trends of the late sixteenth century and the early seventeenth, which increasingly separated people from the natural world and placed renewed stress on intellectual reason and abstract measured analysis of the world. During the medieval period the term 'individual' had referred to the person as indivisible from God's world (Palsson 1996: 65), permeated by the properties of specific places such as sacredness. Contact with unseen features of the world, like spirits, might affect a part of the person like the mind or soul, and provide different sensations and perspectives. During and after the Renaissance more emphasis was placed on the unit, on the individual, which now could be more fully divided from the world – but not internally divided. Increasingly the individual was seen as distinct from the rest of the physical world and indivisible as an integral unit. The human mind and soul were increasingly seen as contained by the human body (see Chapter 5 for further discussion of medieval and post-medieval bodies and personhood).

The individual was redefined and reproduced through historical conditions that stressed an internalized will and unique sense of self located solely within the body (Bordo 1987: ch. 4). The elevation of internal thought and the fixed, constant perspective of the individual can be seen in the development of conventions for perspective painting. During the medieval period artworks had little sense of perspective, depicting rather the significant connections between figures in a story. The same figure could feature several times in one work (Bordo 1987: 63). This allowed the artist to depict *multiple* relationships between that person and the world, and tell a story. From the fifteenth century, perspective – location in measured time and space – prioritized singular interpretations, and had come to replace embedded existence in places and events, absorption in the world. Portraiture, novels, recording dates of birth and death, diaries, headstones, private rooms, quiet introspection and scientific research, and mass-consumed private possessions were all social technologies through which notions and experiences of individuality were produced through the post-medieval period (e.g. Bordo 1987; Deetz 1977; Miller 1987: 161–2). These can all be referred to as components in a 'technology of the self' (Foucault 1984; cf. Battaglia 1995: 4–5), a technology that supported the internalization of the self and the individuation of the person. In focusing on the faculties of the mind, and on the study of external objects, the intelligensia of the sixteenth and seventeenth centuries created an 'internal space' for thought and reflection – the mind – separated from the external world of things. Descartes's idea that mental work was required to understand existence stood at odds with the medieval world-view where engaging with the world involved 'merging with rather than domination of the object, understanding as coded in the heart rather than the head, participatory, nonpatriarchal language' (Bordo 1987: 9). In the post-medieval climate the senses, the body and the soul no longer related directly to their participation in worldly events but were subject to the will of the individual. Genius was no longer a visiting spirit or epiphany which affected people, places and events, but instead was a feature of specific individuals like Leonardo da Vinci (Bordo 1987: 53; Wolff 1981). Attributes of personhood that had been embedded in the world, then, like the self, became increasingly contained within the body. While invisible or spiritual qualities were embedded in places and events in the medieval world, like sacred relics or places with the power to heal, these capacities were increasingly accredited only to human agency (see Chapter 5). This trend individuated the person from the world in what Susan Bordo (1987) has described as a 'drama of parturition' from nature. It was through this process of separation between person and world that thought came to be located in the mind of the person and the mind fastened to the brain. Difference of opinion became a matter of subjectivity, an expression of the subject's singularity and distinctiveness evident in their personal style and choices. Individual character was emergent from within each individual, rather than a result of, for instance, the coalescence of humours passing through them.

As the person became distinct from the natural world, from events tied to places, and from affecting spirits and conditions, so persons became more indivisible. The modular person, a being of different aspects, became less important as a focus of philosophical thought during the eighteenth and nineteenth centuries. The body largely dropped into the philosophical background, and was appropriated by increasingly specialized medical sciences. As feminist historians have argued, the body (along with nature and the feminine) were rendered as passive and equated with unhelpful and irrational emotion, while the intellectual faculties of the person were masculinized (e.g. Hekman 1990; Irigaray

14

1985; Braidotti 1991; Bordo 1987). Philosophy focused on these masculinized facets (public life, reason, free will, ethics, empirical facts, the existence of God) in the eighteenth, nineteenth and twentieth centuries, and accorded increasing importance to the role of the individual in society. The exercise of individual will – an emergent property of the mind – took the foreground in philosophy, along with considerations of how to mediate between conflicting wills in society. The philosophies of Thomas Hobbes (1588–1679) and Jean-Jacques Rousseau (1712–1778) accentuated the significance of the individual, respectively as a basic 'machine' which built society (a larger machine) or as a naturally unfettered creature constrained by the rules of society (Morris 1991: 14–22; Thomas 2004). The idea of the social contract was postulated as a kind of agreement which individuals entered into in forming this mechanistic society. Society was thought of as a collection of individuals, and as functioning as an organism or machine since that is how each individual worked (see Chapter 5). Ideas like this, where social motivation is seen as originating in the will of individual bodies, which then group together to form a society, fall under the umbrella of methodological individualism. Scholars of the time, like Giambattista Vico (1668–1774), believed that the search for natural laws pioneered by men like Isaac Newton (1642–1727) would lead to the designation of social laws, grounded in human nature. The principle taken up by early social scientists was that individuals acted reciprocally, returning kind with kind, and would agree to treat each other equally. It was the foundation of the 'free market' of western economic theory (Douglas and Ney 1998) which Adam Smith saw as serving individuals, and Karl Marx as enslaving them (Weiner 1992: 28). Strength of will and clarity of reason were key tenets of a successful individual, and therefore of society. In nineteenth-century social evolutionary thought, these features were marks of proper, good people, and would win through in the survival of the fittest, while the poor were clearly lacking in such qualities and would founder if left to themselves (Spencer 1857). This view was exploited in colonialism and the justification of social inequality. Each person therefore consisted of set and natural qualities. By the twentieth century the concepts 'person', 'self', 'body' and 'human being' became almost isomorphic.

Individuality and individualism

Individuality and indivisibility are two key attributes of western personhood, therefore. Historically, western personhood has been compressed within the physical body: the mind sits in the brain, which is part of the body, and the soul or spirit has been predominantly replaced by individuality as the essential spiritual component of each person in an increasingly secular society. Individuality is construed as foundational to human nature and fixed within each person (Cohen 1994). It is seen as a fundamental feature of human nature 'after' which relationships are formed (Strathern 1992a: 22). Like nature, individuality is understood as the origin of diversity (ibid.). Individuality, the self-awareness essential to each distinctive individual, is seen as arising from within each of us, providing us with the will to go on even through considerable odds (Cohen 1994). Individualism refers to the celebration of individuality, and in its present incarnation individualism values individual expression, autonomy, uniqueness, self-determination and freedom to act (Lukes 1973; cf. Cohen 1994). Arguably, the form of individuality that is celebrated by individualism has itself changed over time (Strathern 1992a: ch. 1). However, the trend towards the indivisible person as a fixed and bounded entity has also incorporated the notion of individuality. Here individuality refers to an internal self, the locus of experience and understanding. Without denying past people individuality in the sense of conscious self-awareness and reflexive agency, it is necessary to recognize that these qualities do not require that the person be indivisible or recognized as predominantly self-authored. There may be different aspects of the person which provide the person with more than one self, and these features may emerge only in certain contexts (see Chapter 5).

The individual as a construct

Our contemporary conception of the individual as indivisible is an influential construct, which has been acted on, reflected upon and revised in everyday experience over the last few centuries. However, there are still times when more relational personhood is brought to the fore when individuals recognize their debts to others and the effects that others' actions have on them, or the conflicting forces within them, or the way that an experience provides a new and unexpected understanding of things. The indivisibility of the individual is a construct, but an important one that pervades our lives and that we bear in mind when we act in the routines of daily life (Butler 1993; Fowler 2000; cf. Riches 2000: 670). From the mid-twentieth century people were increasingly more likely to be called by their first names than surnames (Strathern 1992a: 17–18), during what we would see as a period of 'increasing' individuality. Yet later-twentieth-century individuals were also individualized through social institutions like schools and workplaces, and through consumerism. These engagements make us aware of our boundaries and limitations, aware that we are at once equal and also distinctive, yet also show us to be in some ways evidently unequal, with uncertain boundaries, and subject to conflicting desires. The public presentation of personhood is, however, one of a unique, distinct, self-contained and well-defined individual identity. Commonly, what is a shifting, coping, learning personhood is projected as a fixed totalized individual (cf. Moore 1994: 35). There are other ways to be individuals which do not accentuate the bounded unity of the person (as indivisibility does), nor value the uniqueness and self-determination of each person above the relationships and forces that compose each person (as individualism does). Our specific understanding of individuals and of individuality is coloured by contemporary individualism, and is therefore heavily implicated in it (for archaeological debates over this entanglement, see Meskell 1999: ch. 1; Tarlow 2000; Thomas 2000b).

17

Moving beyond the construct

Archaeological routes

Archaeologists have attempted to unravel this entanglement in various ways. On the one hand, it is possible to study past individuals and give a rich account of the multiple relations in which each individual engaged, placing this within appropriate cultural contexts and considering those lives against a myriad of others (e.g. Hodder 2000; Meskell 1999; Robb 2002). In some contexts it is possible to study the configuration and generation of personhood itself through textual and pictorial media, and account for indigenous understandings of body, person and spiritual or mental features of personhood (e.g. Meskell 1999: ch. 3; Joyce 2000). Alongside this – or as in prehistoric European contexts, in place or pursuit of this – it is possible to study trends in practices through which personhood is constituted alongside the inhabitation of specific material worlds (e.g. Brück 2001a; Chapman 1996, 2000; Dobres 1999; Fowler 2001; Joyce 2000; Thomas 1996). Approaches focusing on trends in action and conceptions of personhood are generally more concerned with how personhood in the past differed from indivisible personhood and contemporary individualism than with focusing on individual lives, though these need not be completely incompatible. One major strand of research into past experience that directly concerns us here is the investigation of 'being in the world' (e.g. Edmonds 1997; Gosden 1994; Thomas 1996; Tilley 1994; cf. Ingold 1993, 2000e). These approaches attend to the way that human experience is immersed in relationships with other people, with things, and place, through tasks and activities. Strategies of action through which people are mutually authored have also come to the fore, alongside analysis of cultural patterns in social relations that do not operate by individualizing people (e.g. Chapman 2000). While Western society is not the only one to have stressed individuality, to recognize a concept of the individual, or exhibit a form of individualism (Bloch 1989: 18), a focus on these traits should not be presumed to be sole or ascendant features of personhood in all past contexts. The approaches explored in this book are therefore a necessary step in considering the full range of factors relevant to past lives. It would be a significant limitation to the archaeological imagination if, to paraphrase Bloch, we imagine that people are *nothing but* individuals. While we should not divest past people of their individuality, we must also accept that concepts of the person and entwined social technologies existed that did not nurture this feature of human experience. There are ethnographic studies that suggest a wider world of personhood, in which individuals and individuality are a small and sometimes insignificant part.

The value of ethnographic constructs

Different conceptions of personhood are borne in mind by people living in other cultural contexts, and are bound up with the specific practices and technologies that shape their lives. Ethnographers have argued that many of these do not individuate the person as indivisible, nor promote individuality. Instead, person-hood may be relational, so that relationships provide perspectives for people engaged in them. People's identities may change as they move through successive relationships with prey, with their parents, with exchange partners. These positions of person-hood can be occupied by animals and objects, and indeed the movement of objects like gifts may force people to change per-spectives in relation with one another: to now be in debt, or now be owed (Strathern 1999: 239). Relational notions of the person might seem particularly fashionable in academia during the post-modern era, but it is also apparent that far older tradi-tions of thought weigh up the permanence of some aspects of the person against the contextual appearance of others. This is the case in Hindu thought, for instance, where the constant *atman* is present throughout life alongside a more mutable person whose identity is far more contextual and relational (Sax 2002: 10). All of the communities discussed in this book do have notions of a fixed individual feature to the person, such as a notion of individual soul or commemoration of individual biographies. People in these communities are individuated as well as immersed in relations, and are aware of individuality as one attribute of their personhood (for examples of this debate, see Battaglia 1995: 7–11; Carrithers *et al.* 1985; LiPuma 1998; Murray 1993 and Spiro 1993; for an ethnography, see Maschio 1994). However, the other relational and contextual features of personhood are those investigated most closely in this book since they afford archaeologists with a broader understanding of how people can be constituted and what concerns, other than individual interests, might have motivated social interaction. What interests me in this book is the impact that forms of social relations have on the constitution of the person. In the next chapter I will explore ethnographic accounts of how relationships constitute people in contextual ways, and how a change in relationships might have a profound effect on the internal composition and character of a person. Ethnographic accounts of personhood are also western interpretations. However, these accounts seek to recognise local narratives, metaphors, relationships and principles shaping personhood: anthropologists studying personhood write narratives *about* the constructs and narratives that people indigenously relate to both consciously and unconsciously. Arguably, archaeologists studying personhood do something similar. Studies of personhood do not suggest that some humans are or were individuals while others are or were not, but rather illustrate how personal identity can operate in a variety of ways other than *western* individuality. Self-awareness should certainly be presumed for all human persons, but, as we will see, is also often indigenously attributed to non-human persons.

Obviously, then, there should be no hard and fast distinction between 'the west and the rest', and studies of personhood discussed in coming chapters illustrate the flaw in conceptualizing western people as fixed and bounded individuals as much as they demonstrate the problems in imagining western personhood as an absolute match for non-western conceptions. Each person is frequently permeated by outside influences and internally divided, and the idea that this is not the case for western individuals is itself part of the illusion of western personhood. Individuality and indivisibility form a lens through which we observe our own lives, but of course there are other ways to make sense of the plural relationships that make us who we are. By recognizing features of personhood undervalued in the west, through ethnography and through archaeology, we may also come to perceive some of the features of our own lives that are obscured by emphasis on the individual. Modern individuals are, to some degree, still relational persons. Equally, while the individual as a biographical unit remains a key feature of personhood, within any cultural context this attribute may only emerge to the fore on rare occasions, and be utterly rejected in others. The presentation of the person is not necessarily an expression of individuality 'from the inside', but an interactive affair dependent on the perceptions of others. In communities where personhood is stressed as a feature of the community (e.g. where a clan is a person; see Chapter 2) it may not be the individual that is the locus of diversity, innovation or decision-making, but a collective person. Houses or clans may constitute the 'moral person'. Uniqueness and innovation are features of clans, expressed through its members. Furthermore, and perhaps more significantly for archaeologists, not all persons in the community are necessarily human, and an emphasis on the individual neglects the role of other social agents accorded personhood (like ghosts, spirits, houses, axes, standing stones), whether these seem real or presumed to contemporary archaeologists. Clearly then, an archaeology of personhood is quite a different project from an archaeology of the lives of specific past individuals, although the two need not be mutually exclusive.

Conclusion

If we recognize individuality as a natural feature of human beings, then, I submit, we should also see relationality and dividuality in the same light. People depend upon the ability to see things from other points of view, people are tugged by multiple concerns, are conflicted, and may lose themselves in experiences and activities. Our predominant conception of the person has a history and context, one that has only been sketched roughly here and that

21

prioritizes a constancy and boundedness to the person (see Thomas, 2004, for a fuller discussion). There were periods of time when European individuals did not exist exactly as they do now, and when belief, reason, will and cause and effect did not emanate from people but were embedded in the world along with people. Concepts of ownership and belonging have also changed through the European past, and with them concepts of the relationships between people, land, animals and things. The development of indivisible personhood and individualism in Europe did not follow the same pattern as relationships that unfolded between people and worlds elsewhere. Past conceptions and experiences of personhood can extend well beyond the indivisible person, and individuality is only one feature of a person in any context. The key features of our predominant understanding of personhood do not paint the full picture of personhood anywhere in the world, and are gradually being bleached in our own society by awareness of the more relational facets of personhood. It has been necessary to feed the archaeological imagination by supplying new angles to our understanding of personhood, reflecting a wider range of human diversity. Exactly how archaeologists have done this, and the ethnographies they have drawn on, forms the basis of remaining chapters.

2

PERSONHOOD AND IDENTITY
Theoretical frameworks

People are modular: they are composites of different substances, and of different features such as the body, mind and soul. This chapter considers some cultural comparisons in personhood suggesting that people are configured in historically specific ways. This chapter traces the practices and knowledges involved in two instances of relational 'dividual' personhood, one Indian and one Melanesian, through examination of ethnographic studies. The inseparability of personhood and other factors of identity, like gender and caste, is also discussed. It is argued that these intersect in culturally specific ways, but that trends can be perceived in the principles structuring social relations and personhood which may be useful in interpreting past societies where similar forms of transactions, transformations and interaction to those discussed here may be inferred.

Personhood and relationships beyond individuality: dividuality, partibility and permeability

This section reviews ethnographic interpretations of personhood in India and Melanesia, and illustrates how we can understand people as dividual and composite, as permeable and as partible. Each of these constructed terms will be explained through analysis of social transactions between persons, and are presented as alternative technologies in configuring personhood to those producing indivisible people. This does not imply that these people do not have individuality or are not individuals, but that they are also something more besides individuals. They live through different conceptions of personhood that anthropologists have devised these terms to understand.

Dividual personhood in India

In historic Europe the late medieval person was primarily understood as a merging of parts temporarily contained within the body (the body consisted of organs and humours, and the person consisted of mind, body and soul). Identifying the person as a series of parts emphasizes what anthropologists call the *dividual* nature of the person, which is the precise opposite of the indivisible person. Dividuals are composites, and their components originate outside of the person (e.g. are provided by the bodies of both parents on conception). The term was coined by McKim Marriott in his study of Indian personhood and caste (Marriott 1976). Marriott examined how substances are transmitted from one body to another, one person to another, and one caste to another. Marriott refers to these as 'substance-codes', since the substance, its form and its effect are inseparable. Examples of substance-codes would be blood, alcohol, cooked food, money, and even knowledge. Each substance-code is valued differently, from gross material like cooked food to subtle 'substance-codes' like knowledge or words. Each substance can be transmuted into another; food once eaten will produce faeces; cremation refines the body into subtler substance-codes, freeing the soul. Throughout life, each person is internally divided and composed of many different substance-codes at once. These can be extended out of the person through exchanges, and given to others. Some substance-codes are gross and hot (e.g. alcohol and the meat of wild animals), while others are cool and subtle (e.g. money, grain). Hot substances stress maleness, so absorbing them masculinizes the person. Giving and receiving these substances affects a person internally, and colours the whole of their social identity including gender and caste. Those who exchange hot substances are frequent exchangers, with a high turnover of essences, and are seen as excitable, unstable and of low caste. Conversely, those who exchange cool, subtle essences do so infrequently, and are typically merchants or artisans. Caste and personhood are absolutely dependent on transaction, and these transactions are carried out according to what practices are deemed appropriate or effective by any caste. In sum, the dividual person is able to process the substances of the world within their person, and these essences also make up the person. However, unlike the essences of the indivisible western individual (e.g. our genetic material, which can only be transmitted in reproduction) these essences can be continually circulated, monitored, transformed – indeed the attainment of personhood depends upon it. Giving and receiving between people alters each person internally. 'By Indian modes of thought, what goes on *between* actors are the same connected processes of mixing and separation that go on *within* actors' (Marriott 1976: 109, original emphases). Substance-codes therefore coalesce in people's bodies, but are also inseparable from the outside world: they are kept in constant circulation. Dividual people are the constantly changing products of social interactions between themselves and others. Each component is therefore the manifestation of a relationship, as each substance-code has been acquired through social interaction.

Dividual and partible personhood in Melanesia

[Melanesian p]ersons are frequently constructed as the plural and composite site of the relationships that composed them. The singular person can be imagined as a social microcosm.

(Strathern 1988: 13–14)

Marilyn Strathern's (1988) study of Highland New Guinea society describes how Melanesian people exist as 'dividual' and 'partible' persons. Strathern's work contends that Melanesian personhood is not like that of western individuals – both in the sense of the structure of the person and also in terms of the motivating concerns and forms of agency behind personal interaction. Strathern argued that Melanesian persons are composed out of relations between others (e.g. both parents), and the ongoing relationships each person engages in. People are multiply-authored. The dividual feature of the person stresses that each person is a composite of the substances and actions of others, which means that each person encompasses multiple constituent things and relations received from other people. Internal composition depends on external relations, and relationships are condensed into physical substances or objects: anything that can be given away. A dividual person contains within them components from the whole community: we could say they share blood with all other members of the community (Mosko 1992: 702–6). If we imagine that the blood of every person is a slightly different colour, then each Melanesian dividual would contain one drop of different coloured blood for everyone in the community. However, people cannot marry the same blood. If a dividual were to marry with someone else it would be necessary to externalize that piece of their person which originated in their potential spouse's family (Mosko 1992: 703–6). Some internalized part of the person must be detached, and returned to the other family via one of its members; this is represented in Figure 2.1. This is partibility, decomposing the person to allow new relationships. Partibility means that the person decreases in scale slightly, while the part they give away is encompassed by another (Figure 2.1). Whereas each person, as a product of relations between all community members, normally encapsulates components from the whole community, partibility allows them to 'scale down' the size of the community they encapsulate (Mosko 1992: 710) so that they only contain components from a single family or a single clan. This opens the way for new relations to be formed with the excluded community. The part given will be returned, though in a different form (e.g. many pigs rather than one axe), and again internalized. Therefore, the Melanesian person is both dividual and partible, though sometimes one feature sublimates the other. Partibility occurs most notably in marriage exchanges, in ceremonial exchanges, and, following death, during the final

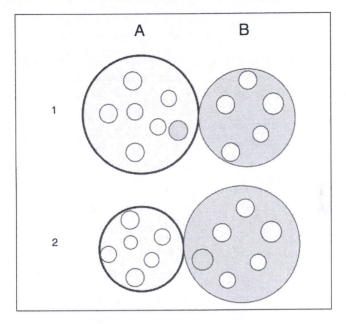

Figure 2.1 Graphic depiction of partibility. 1. Part of person A is owed to B.
2. That part is externalized through a gift and absorbed by B.
A has reduced scale to externalize B's family from A's dividual
person. This part will be returned through a different gift object
in the future.

decomposition of the person (Mosko 1992). It is not only substances which are part of each person, but also objects: we can
think of things in a dividual world as always part of one person
or another. As we will see in the next chapter, objects are actually
parts of more than one person in dividual understandings of
personhood: they link two people together intimately. As exem-
plified in Box 2.1, these may be objects or even animals that we
would see as external to the person, but in Melanesia are incorporated into the person.

Box 2.1 The 'Are'are person

The ethnographer Daniel de Coppet has studied personhood and exchanges among the 'Are'are of the Solomon Islands, Melanesia (de Coppet 1981; Barraud *et al*. 1994). He argues that the 'Are'are consider the world of living things to contain three elements which are encapsulated in the human person. These are translated roughly as 'body', 'breath' and 'image':

> The three constituent elements of the 'Are'are universe are unequally distributed among different beings. Cultivated plants are generally considered to have only body; domesticated pigs, body and breath; and humans, body, breath and image.
>
> (Barraud *et al*. 1994: 53)

Image is also a quality of the 'Are'are ancestors, and can be found in shell goods. Key spiritual characteristics of a person may therefore also be contained within things and animals. Gathering these together may add these qualities to a person. This is rather different to the western formulation of mind, body and soul where the mind and soul are conventionally exclusive to the human body. Objects can also be encapsulated by an 'Are'are person, and become a part of that person, though they do not necessarily become a part of the body. The elements which compose the 'Are'are person are distributed throughout the social world; they are to be found in the things which people grow, cultivate, rear and, most vitally, exchange. In other words, the qualities to be found in persons are found elsewhere in the world, in objects and plants and animals. Each person is formed through their circulation of these things in their lifetime; the more pigs they can gather up, the greater their breath, for example. In a funerary rite all of these different elements

continued on facing page

of the person will be brought together around the deceased. This act brings the person together. The implication is that while alive the person is distributed throughout the social and material world, and only becomes a whole person temporarily during this mortuary rite. All of the things that the person encapsulates are brought together and made explicit for everyone to see. They are then divided up again and these parts are redistributed through mortuary exchanges.

Ceremonial gift exchange in Highland New Guinea is a good example of partibility. Gift exchange requires that objects be extracted out of the person who had previously encapsulated them, so that part can be given to another person, forming a dual relation. A part of the person is removed, and is absorbed by another (see Figure 2.2). The partible person is a partial *version* of that person, in which the extracted part is presented as the whole. The gift appears to be an end product, a whole and single thing, but it was actually multiply-authored (Strathern

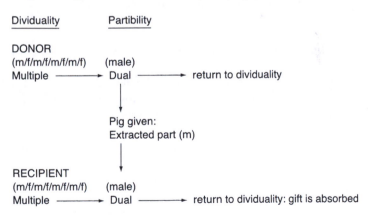

It is during this act that the donor presents the gift as a single feature of their person, a unitary version of a multiple person.

Figure 2.2 The partibility of the singular person. Example given: male–male (single sex) exchange.

1988: 159). Pigs are often such gifts. A pig is reared jointly by a man and wife, and so is itself a dividual entity which has been multiply-authored. Yet the pig is encapsulated by the man who extracts it from the domestic group, then extracts it from himself and gives it to another. The man is able to dispose of a part of himself by giving the pig, and also acts as one part of the group that made the pig (his family, and his clan). In offering the gift as a single feature of his person, he temporarily presents a unitary version of himself: the giver of this pig who stands for his family. In giving a gift a single relationship between donor and recipient is temporarily accentuated above all the others that composed the gift and both people. That relationship defines the gift, and also defines the giver, both of which appear in singular form even though they are multiply-constituted:

> In Hagen, it is emphatically the achievement of men's ceremonial exchange system that they transform this [wealth] into a singular entity for themselves: wealth comes to stand for that part of themselves which is then construed as their whole self, their prestige.
>
> (Strathern 1988: 159)

So, while partibility presents the person as a singular entity, this does not compose an indivisible individual. Partibility actually decomposes a dividual temporarily (Mosko 1992: 702), and presents only one facet of their usually multiple person. With partible people, the act of separating creates a distinct – but not complete (Strathern 1988: 185) – temporary identity: '[t]he general enchainment of relations means that persons are multiply constituted. There is no presumption of an innate unity: such an identity is only created to special, transient effect' (Strathern 1988: 165).

Partibility is particular to the exchange of gifts or people, which, Strathern argues, are equivalents for each other. Substances, rather than objects or persons, are transmitted in a rather different process directly between dividuals, and may be grown within dividuals (Strathern 1988: 207–19). We will trace the implications of these two sets of exchanges in Chapters 3 and 5. People repeatedly fluctuate between their ongoing dividual nature as persons composed and sustained by multiple relations, and their partible nature as people who can dispose of parts of themselves that are in fact the product of multiple relations with others. A singular person is usually dividual, and this is taken for granted (Strathern 1988: 276, fig. 4). In Strathern's view, then, the Melanesian person is always modulating, always shifting identities, as they move through different spheres of relations. 'Social life consists in a constant movement from one state to another, from a unity (manifested collectively or singly) to that unity split or paired with respect to another' (Strathern 1988: 14). Each of these positions provides a different perspective for all concerned in the event. In making these transformations people are also always changing scale, so that their person incorporates parts from their family, their clan, and even other clans. Since people therefore exist at a range of different scales, and since objects are extracted from people like people are extracted from clans in marriage exchanges, clans and gifts are also persons. We will return to this.

Permeable personhood in India

Cecilia Busby (1997) has recently commented on Strathern's reading of dividual and partible personhood, and stressed that while these principles structuring personhood are relevant to Melanesia, they do not apply in southern India. In her studies of the Marianad fishing community in southern India she argued that the dividual persons there were more *permeable* than partible, and did not engage in partible relations (see Table 2.1). It is worth mentioning that while Busby's ethnography is of a Latin Catholic village, not a Hindu community as Marriott's was, she argues for strong similarities between them (Busby 1997: 276, n. 1). While money, food, alcohol and bodily substances (like blood and saliva) were circulated between people as Marriott suggested, Busby argues that these were not parts extracted from a person but merely substance-codes extended out from them (Busby 1997: 273).

The flows of substance which move between Mukkavar persons are issued out of their person, but are not separable and identifiable parts that must be isolated and returned to others (Busby 1997: 275). These flows are media through which relations with others are generated, and used in altering the composition of the person according to specific doctrines of practice. It is in the transaction and manipulation of substance-codes that personal identity is generated. Whereas in Melanesia the gender and significance of the gift depends on who is doing the giving, and which 'part' of them the gift is standing for, in India the gender and substance of the gift is essential (Busby 1997: 272). In India each substance-code has a fixed gender, meaning and effect (Busby 1997: 271, 275). Consequently there is no 'ambiguous' substance-code (Busby 1997: 273): dealing with more hot substance-codes accent-uates maleness, while dealing with more cold substance-codes accentuates femaleness. However, in Melanesia, substances may be ambiguous, so that, for instance, semen may be seen as milk, and vice versa (Strathern 1988: 214). People, things and sub-stances are re-gendered by the relations that distinguish and acti-vate them. However, as in Melanesia, Indian personhood also fluctuates throughout life, going through different degrees of permeability. Strathern's interpretation of Melanesian partible personhood does not therefore apply in southern India, where we could say the person is instead conceived of as dividual in a permeable way. In partible relations one part of the person is replaced with another. In permeable relations the quantity and strength of each substance-code is altered, but no parts are really removed even if their size and ratios change.

Therefore, anthropologists have identified at least two versions of dividual personhood in these instances, with two different principles behind social interaction. Partibility operates through isolating and extracting parts of the person, and permeability circulates quantities of substance between discrete yet pervious people. Both exhibit features different from the indivisibility that characterizes the western individual.

Table 2.1 Differences between partible personhood in Melanesia and permeable personhood in India (based on interpretation of Busby 1997)

Dividual and partible (Melanesia)	Dividual and permeable (southern India)
A person is a collection of relations, any of which may be temporarily brought to the fore. Qualities can be added and extracted.	A person is fundamentally a collection of relations, and is a bounded being from whom qualities cannot be fully extracted though ratios may change.
Persons identify relations which are objectified; as animals, objects, body parts, substances, etc. These can be externalised through separation or incorporated through encompassment. As well as being objectified they may be personified.	Substance-codes can permeate the 'fluid boundaries' of the person. Flows of substance extend from persons, they are not objectified as a specific part of the person.
Things fluctuate between being male and female, and singly and multiply gendered, depending on the context of their use.	Substance-codes have fixed properties (e.g. hot or cold).
Personhood is highly relational, and identities are performed or presented.	Personhood is relational, but is also strongly substantial.

Reconciling trends in dividual and individual personhood

It has been suggested that dividual forms of personhood like those prevalent in parts of India, and particularly Melanesia, are radically different from western individual personhood – including by archaeologists (e.g. Fowler 2000, 2002; Thomas 2000a, 2000b, 2002 – cf. Meskell 1999: ch. 1; Tarlow 2000 for critiques; and Chapman 2000; Fowler 2001, 2003; Jones 2002a: 161–2 for refinements). An important critique of this approach is that we should not create a firm division between persons in the west and 'the rest' of the world. Edward LiPuma's (1998) analysis of Melanesian and western personhood attempts to resolve the problems caused by this distinction (cf. Battaglia 1995). LiPuma starts by pointing out that our understanding of western individuals and Melanesian dividuals are constructions of our own making (see Chapter 1). These classic distinctions portray western individuals as bounded indivisible entities possessing fixed innate character traits, as alienated from their world, as engaging in relations of capitalist possession towards things, animals and land, and as standing in opposition to society (cf. LiPuma 1998: 58–9). Such conventions also present dividuals as authored by interaction with others, as integrated within their world, as inseparable from the gifts they give, and as a microcosm of society. In fact, LiPuma argues, there are individual and dividual facets to all people:

> it is a misunderstanding to assume either that the social emerges out of individual action, a powerful strain in Western ideology which has seeped into much of its scientific epistemology, or that the individual ever completely disappears by virtue of indigenous forms of relational totalisation (such as those posited for certain New Guinea societies). It would seem rather that *persons emerge precisely from that tension between dividual and individual aspects/relations*. And the terms and conditions of this tension, and thus the kind (and range) of persons that is produced will vary historically.
>
> (LiPuma 1998: 57)

For LiPuma, then, each person negotiates a tension between dividual and individual characteristics, and, in all societies, personhood emerges from the constant reconciling of one with the other. In some contexts, like modern Europe, individual features are accentuated, while in others, like contemporary Melanesia, dividual features are accentuated – but these are *dominant* features, not factors which completely repress or override the other (Fowler 2000). Within our own society there are spheres of action which usually accentuate the individual (e.g. academic examinations) and those which stress relational, dividual facets (e.g. funerals). LiPuma stresses that societies place different emphases on the dividual and individual facets of personhood: in the west individuality is of primary concern in the definition of laws, rights and social *mores*, while in Melanesia dividuality has taken the foreground in cultural logic, personal expectation and social interaction (LiPuma 1998: 63–4).

There are clearly no cross-culturally universal patterns in how tensions between dividual and individual facets of personhood are negotiated. Hindu gift-giving may accentuate dividuality if it is profuse and no gifts are received in return (Marriott 1976: 131). Equally, reception without giving may accentuate more individual aspects of personhood. It would often seem that dividuality and permeability are accentuated when exchanges are most frequent. In Melanesia, however, dividuality is accentuated on a daily basis, since people are multiple products of others all the time, while the person may be temporarily individuated as partible by gift-giving. A woman marrying into a clan is particularized as a partible feature passing between two clans: while she is presented as an individual being, a single component of the clan, her individuality *sensu* Cohen (1994) may have relatively little to do with the matter. In Strathern's text individuals emerge from dividuality as partible people where one aspect of identity is presented as a whole self. Exactly what is presented depends upon the context. Strathern also describes how a biographical individual *does* emerge as history recorded in the body (Strathern 1988: 282), yet this feature of personhood is not presented as frequently or as strongly as others. In a dividual state a person is full of potential, and is plural; in a partible state they are defined by a present relation; individual histories may selectively sum up the history of these conditions. Dividuality here exists in tension with partibility as well as individuality: this recognition gives us a frame to understand personal motivations in social actions. Melanesian practices, Melanesian ways of negotiating personhood, mediate social concerns and give shape to the person, colouring their desires and intentions. While a tension between different concerns over personhood do exist, then, the exact principles that hold sway and the practices that mediate between them are culturally specific. The tension between individual and dividual is therefore negotiated in different arenas, and in culturally specific ways.

LiPuma's perspective is a valuable starting point in framing personhood as a negotiation between different concerns. However, there are historical and cultural trends in the principles through which these tensions are negotiated. In India degrees of dividuality and individuality emerge through the strategies people employ in their exchanges. These strategies change throughout life and are dependent on membership of age groups, cults and caste (see pp. 44–7). In Melanesia personal concerns are shaped by a community-oriented moral code which does not stress individuality. Each person internalizes the community rather than standing in opposition to it. The person is dividual, and partibility is the key mechanism through which multiply-constituted people are reconfigured throughout their lives. Individuality is increasingly influential due to colonial contact, and this has led to an increase in sorcery accusations since individualistic behaviour is deemed anti-social (LiPuma 1998). In the west the person is primarily individual, but the principles of indivisibility and uniqueness cannot entirely override the influence of our more dividual features. Permeability and partibility are, then, the core principles in two culturally specific fields of personhood. But in an analytical sense archaeologists may consider that the practices and principles associated with partibility and permeability may be analogous to those practised by past communities. This is at least as plausible as the idea that past people were indivisible individuals. The question can be partly resolved through study of the past practices and social technologies that accompanied conceptions of the person in a given context. Present practices that accompany dividual personhood are therefore used in forming analogies for personhood in the past. Clearly, a focus on strategies of transaction, exchange media, transformations, and social technologies in general provides the most fruitful avenue in interpreting past modes of personhood. The media of past activities afford archaeologists the chance to study how personhood was produced through features of social interaction like partibility and permeability.

The production of personhood

Forms of dividual personhood in the past were probably different to those in both Melanesia and India. However, similar principles and conceptions to those structuring permeable or partible personhood might have existed in past communities. Although the cultural significance of practices like permeability or partibility cannot be divorced from the practice itself, such practices are not conceptions of personhood in themselves. For example, permeability does not by itself form the religious basis for Hindu personhood: Hinduism provides that. Yet Indian Christians are dividual and permeable too (Busby 1997). Rather than comparing partibility and permeability directly as though they were whole systems of ways to be persons, then, we can consider these as mechanisms and processes vital to the formulation of personhood. They perpetuate a shape to relationships that support certain trends in personhood, and gender, ethnicity, and so on. These patterns of action are structuring principles: the principles that structure activity (Barrett 2000: 63–4). In our interactions with one another, and with the things of the world, we pursue social strategies that activate the structuring principles in different ways. These principles are visible in what people do; who they exchange with, what they give, what effects these exchanges have. Structuring principles are ways of doing things, then, that involve interpretations and reconfigurations of structural conditions; the material and historical circumstances in which people live. A concept of personhood, alongside the things of the material world left by past activities themselves shaped by structuring principles, would be a feature of such structural conditions. People do not simply reproduce concepts of personhood in what Meskell (1999: 20) rightly critiques as a 'fax transmission' view of cultural determinism. Rather, people engage both with these conceptions *and* with the previous practices through which they have been negotiated in the pursuit of desired social effects (see also Butler 1993). In short, they live within modes of personhood in ways negotiated through interaction. Their acts may be orthodox or unorthodox, and may or may not have the desired effect in attaining a certain kind of identity, a certain state of personhood. Their acts may also lead to revisions in the way the practices generating personhood are conducted and the way that personhood is conceptualized. Therefore, no mode of personhood is static, and people do not blindly reproduce them. However, both the conception of personhood and the practices that sustain it are culturally specific. Here we review why this is so, and how this realization helps in interpreting personhood in the past.

Bodies and social technologies

Distinctive bodies are produced through cultural practices like tattooing, body-building, feasting and fasting, beautification, and daily patterns of work. These bodies are monitored by society, and as much as they are produced by individuals they are produced through patterns of action and interaction (e.g. Bourdieu 1977, 1990; Butler 1990, 1993, 1994; Connerton 1990; Foucault 1977). While there are certain similarities between all human bodies, understandings and experiences of the body vary by social background, cultural practices, ethnicity, gender, sexuality and other factors of identity. For example, Moira Gatens (1992) argues that a female athlete may share a sense of embodiment with a male athlete more readily than with a female office worker. We may recognise different types of body not only by what sexual organs they have but also by how tanned they are, or whether they 'pump iron', how they are dressed or how they move, or whether they are tattooed and how heavily (Featherstone 2000; Turner 1984). Each biological human body is therefore produced through a set of cultural practices appropriate to certain social contexts.

There are different cultural trends in embodiment (Csordas 1999). Archaeologists therefore need to consider how past bodies were produced, and the practices that generated and revalued those bodies from conception, birth and childhood, through adulthood and even after death. While these trends operate through the human body, the metaphors and principles entailed also permeate the material world. For example, marking a Polynesian body through tattooing might be directly analogous to marking the land through rock art production, and the stab-decoration of pottery (Rainbird 2002). For this reason it is necessary to understand the processes that produce bodies and people as shaping the world too: it is impossible to separate a study of bodies from a study of social technologies (Dobres 1999: 149–57). Partibility involves not only relations between people, but relations with things, places and the cosmos at large. On one level this due to the ability of metaphors to move across contexts, to apply to people and things. But on a more significant level social technologies, which are sets of transformative practices, themselves shape the people who engage in them (e.g. Brück 2001a; Chapman 1996: 207–8; Dobres 1999: 19; Jones 2002: 89–90; Lakoff and Johnson 1980). Schools, prisons, and other social institutions play key roles in shaping our bodies as a technology of the self (Foucault 1977), and, as already argued, there have been specific technologies like diaries, novels, portraiture and private bedrooms that have all been brought to bear in producing historically specific modes of personhood. Devisch (1993) describes, in an example from the Congo, how the Yaka see the body as being like cloth on a loom, actively woven throughout life, yet bearing a biographical tapestry. The metaphor not only describes the body as a locus of social relations, but also the kind of process through which the body is generated: the experience of being in social relations is like the work of weaving at the loom. It is through working on a loom that Yaka people come to understand life as being like weaving. The gestures and attitudes that are employed in practices like weaving are used in crafting social relationships, and to frame spiritual relations with the cosmos (Tilley 1999: 40). Personhood is therefore effected through our daily interactions with things, with each other, and with the world at large. Social interaction and personhood are therefore intelligible through technological activity. We have already seen that in order to understand Melanesian personhood the process of gift exchange must be understood, for instance. Throughout this book we will see that while human bodies are vital nexuses of personhood, personhood can also be interpreted from other material remains.

Box 2.2 Personhood, metaphor and technologies of the body: middle and late Bronze Age southern Britain (1800–900 BC)

Working from the starting point that dividuality was a key feature of Bronze Age life, Joanna Brück has compared the transformative processes applied to the human body after death with the treatment of houses, pottery, bronzes, grain and quernstones (Brück 1995, 1999, 2001a). In so doing she has given a description of the dominant principles structuring personhood in the middle and late Bronze Age. During the middle Bronze Age 'token' cremation deposits were common – these were deposits consisting of only a fraction of the entire cremated remains of the dead. Fragmented human bones, particularly skull fragments, were sometimes made into objects like pendants. The body was therefore not treated as a whole, but broken up and redistributed to different locations and perhaps among different groups of people: we could say that bodies became gifts to be circulated. Brück draws out parallels between this treatment of the human body with the fragmentation of pottery and metalwork. Pots were smashed and ground up, and fragments used to temper the next generation of pottery. Some potsherds and human remains were spread on the land along with other waste products, making it fertile. The cereals harvested were also ground up to make bread or alcohol that would be ingested into the human body. Some cereals would be stored for planting in the next season. Bronze objects were scrapped, and some fragments were recycled in smelting further objects. Quernstones were used to crush grains to make bread, perhaps to grind up potsherds for

continued on facing page

temper, and perhaps even to disintegrate the bones of the dead. Bread, pots, bronzes and human bodies were all fired or cremated in transforming them from one state to another. The body of each was broken down to reproduce a new generation of bodies. Quernstones themselves were not broken, since they were the 'anvil' on which other bodies were broken, reworked and recycled, but were often buried in significant locations around houses when those houses were themselves 'decommissioned' or abandoned.

The social lives of people and things were therefore cyclical, and followed similar patterns. Fragmentation and heat were key elements in the transformation of each material or body. Remains of things were incorporated into the bodies of the next generation of those objects, while human remains were immersed into the community and throughout the landscape. A regenerative principle was in operation, re-cycling substances and maintaining the continual repro-duction of people, things and places. Brück's approach provides an account of the overall principles pervading middle and later Bronze Age society, including personhood. She argues that the social technologies of potting, land husbandry and metalworking were also technologies of the self, conjoining person and world (Brück 2001a). This approach illustrates that understanding personhood requires interpreting social practices in the transformation of bodies and objects, and the circulation of substances: one of the core themes traced in this book.

Patterns in practices are not identities in themselves, but are the means through which identities are shaped and perpetuated. A particular exchange format might be appropriate to a mode of personhood, but does not by itself produce personhood. Particular strategies for deploying that format are pursued by people in generating both their own person and the personhood of others. In other words, there are mutually interactive strategies through which personhood is produced, within any overarching logic referred to here as a mode of personhood. Those strategies are shaped not only by the desire to produce a certain kind of personhood, but also by desires particular to other social interests like age or gender.

Strategic interactions: negotiating personhood alongside other features of identity

All features of identity are contextual – the kind of person one may be in a certain context is quite different from the kind of person one might be in another. This is the case whether or not a fixed individual aspect of the person is accentuated. However, these contexts are themselves events in which different social interests are mediated. Personhood is only fully intelligible in relation to gender, caste, descent and ethnic identity: in fact any features of identity that influence social interaction. Trends in practice like permeability and partibility are central to personhood, but they also provide the mechanisms through which these other features of identity are mediated. In this section I very briefly draw out some of the entanglements between personhood and other features of identity, using gender, age and caste as examples. Kinship and ethnicity are also core issues in personhood, but I will not deal with these explicitly here (see Jones 1997 for a review of recent studies of ethnicity).

Gendering and personhood

The manipulation and transaction of gendered materials and gendered bodies are vital areas of study affecting our understanding of identity as a whole, including personhood. Gender is a fundamental feature of each person (for recent reviews on the relationship between bodies and gendering, see Sørenson 2000; Gosden 1999; Gilchrist 1999). As we have seen in several of the examples discussed so far, the different substances and objects that become a part of the person may be gendered either in a fixed way or relative to their use. In India the circulation of gendered substances alters the overall gender of the person, but gendered identity is immanent in the body. These substances can be socially manipulated so the gender of each person is not completely fixed but is dependent on the control of substance (Busby 1997: 265–7). Control and transmission of gender substance-codes demonstrate personal gender. However, Melanesian materials and bodies are not gendered in this fixed way. Any substance, thing or person may in one context be revealed as male and in another as female, depending on how it is activated, so is latently both. For example, a number of symbols (e.g. flutes) are referred to as penis or breast, or penis or womb (Strathern 1988: 208–15). 'Whether a tube turns out to be a penis or a birth canal depends on how it is and how it has been activated' (Strathern 1988: 128). Both male and female bodies are also ambiguous in this way, dividual combinations of male and female, and their bodies are activated as one or the other according to the relationship taking place. While male and female gendering is the significant feature in many societies, Strathern (1988) argues that single-sex versus cross-sex relationships are the more important factor in conceptualizing Melanesian gender. People move between these relationships continually, gendering their bodies either multiply (as a dividual) or in a dual relationship (in a partible state). Like personhood, gender must be made to appear in one form or another, and this is a constant process. Each object and body is potentially singly gendered (i.e. male or female), or may be multiply gendered (both male and female at once, and potentially also genderless) depending on the relationship it is used to mediate. Some relationships are same-sex, while others are cross-sex, and each activates the gender of a person, substance or thing in a different way.

From an archaeological perspective, it is clear that parts of people, things and material substances might be differently gendered (Moore 1986), either inherently, or relative to the context in which they are activated. The overall gender of the person as a whole might contain a balance of many different influences and substances. The body may be composed of male and female substance derived from each parent. These coalesce in the body, either generically, or forming particular gendered matter. Mortuary practices may, for instance, separate out male bone from female flesh where such identifications are made (Bloch 1982). Different kinds of exchanges may also be gendered, as is the case in some Melanesian contexts where men may supervise marriages and the composition of a person, while women control the decomposition of the person and the recycling of the constitutive essences (e.g. Munn 1986). Gendering, along with the attainment of a certain type of personhood, is effected through engagement in specific practices, such as the generation and transmission of particular substances (e.g. semen). Some persons are able repeatedly to encapsulate both male and female substances, practices and genders in a different way to others (e.g. Hollimon 2000; Prine 2000). Some of these 'third genders' are only temporarily attained, and some practitioners move from one gender to another throughout life. Not all persons in all societies attain a permanent gender, and as we will see not all human beings become full persons or attain an enduring and constant form of personhood. Gender is often achieved as a result of social strategies in action, whether to manipulate gendered substances or to gender the world through relationships. Some of these strategies may deliberately emulate and parody others, producing changing and ambiguous gendered identities (Butler 1993). Much of this contrasts with conventional western ideas about constant individual identity where gender is within the person and a feature of our sexed bodies. Understandings of gender as mutable and forms of relational personhood are therefore co-extensive.

Age and personhood

Ethnographies suggest that people in India are permeated by relationships through the pursuit of certain exchange strategies. Marriott (1976: 131–2) identifies four life stages in which Hindu personhood is reconfigured due to changing exchange strategies. First, studentship, in which people engage in a very low frequency of exchanges, mainly absorbing from their teachers. Second, as a householder, where exchanges are frequent as much must be acquired and this necessitates a high frequency of gift turnover. This accentuates the internal diversity of the person, since they become many things to other people as householders, including, usually, parents. Third, retirement, in which everything possible is given away, and nothing will be received. Pre-existing relations are contained within the dividual person, but new relations are not formed. This is followed by the fourth stage, renunciation, in which the person receives gross media from all members of society, but very little from any one person in particular, and gives only rare punctuations of subtle and highly potent substance-codes. This is the stage that Marriott identifies as most like the western individual person, since the person accumulates goods but is also entirely independent from any benefactor, and also exhibits a status as an accumulator of identities, retaining knowledge about the three previous stages of personhood. Different exchange strategies are therefore crucial to Hindu personhood. Life stages are one of the features that shape these strategies.

Age is also one of the key concepts in understanding person-hood, since a person is conceived and born, and after many life-changing experiences (including death: see Chapter 5) may eventually cease to be a person at all. Exactly when a person is fully considered as such varies culturally, and is an issue that lies at the heart of debates over abortion, for example. Rites of passage to do with age grades are often held throughout life, draw-ing out a new feature of the person and diminishing others, and binding together people of the same age group. Inclusion into certain spheres of the adult world may be the point at which full personhood is attained – in the Punjab, Alvi (2001: 60) states that 'because an unmarried person cannot take part in gift exchange, he or she has no part in constructing the social world'. Funerary rites exhibit extensive gradations by caste, age and married status, so that 'even a grown-up but unmarried person does not receive the full funeral rites' (ibid.). These people can be compared with those in other societies where 'even the majority does not reach the final, complete stages of personhood, like the many among the Tallensi who cannot be called 'nit' ['person' . . .], or those *Jivaro* who did not have an *arutam* encounter' (Alvi 2001: 49). This is made all the stranger to us since animals and objects may be persons in such societies. Alvi is identifying the relational and contingent character of persons here, so that personhood is achieved only on fulfilment of certain conditions. Maschio (1994: 107) describes Rauto puberty rites as 'the attainment of personhood', achieved through access to material culture that conveys personhood. Age is perhaps not the best criteria *per se* for understanding these conditions so much as what people can do given their age, relations and circumstances. A number of archaeological studies have focused on the social construction of age, gender and the life-cycle (e.g. Moore and Scott 1997; Sofaer Derevenski 2000). The differential treatment of the living and dead by age may well mark out differences in personhood, from the exclusion of certain people from full personhood, to the changing social strategies for pursuing personal relations that pertain to certain life stages.

Personhood, caste and religion

Caste often distinguishes different kinds of persons in a fundamental way, so that 'equality in South Asia is thus the sense of belonging to the same category' (Alvi 2001: 51), but sharing the same religion will also bestow that equality to a certain degree. Caste is, however, hierarchical and exclusionary. Relationships of equal exchanges are bounded within one community, and unequal exchanges mark others as of a higher or lower caste (Marriott 1976). Whichever strategy for transferring substance-codes the caste employs is broadly followed by all its members – for instance, whether to give or receive alcohol to or from members of another particular caste. Since alcohol is 'hot' it heats and lubricates the person, catalysing frequent exchanges. To deal excessively in alcohol is to become an excitable person, and one who exchanges frequently. Castes dealing in alcohol will be seen as excitable and as frequent exchangers of gross substance-codes. So the characteristics of one's caste are as one's own personhood, and the caste is the most basic and expansive social unit. But membership of religious cults and other affiliations influence the type of exchange strategy a person pursues, the kind of substance-code that will be exchanged, and who it can be exchanged with, and therefore the internal composition of the person (Marriott 1976: 130). The composition of a Shiva devotee might be more similar to another Shiva cult member than to another member of the same caste who follows a different cult. Caste, religion and ethnicity are all contextual, and different emphases are placed on these affiliations depending on the social context. That such changes are possible illustrates the great diversity of identities even within what seems a rigid caste system. Nonetheless, identifying the principles that characterize personhood – in this case the transmission of substance-codes between dividual and permeable people – was something that Marriott (1976) found vital in understanding the Hindu caste system.

Summary: personhood, identity and context

Trends in social practice exist alongside specific concepts of the person in modes of personhood. These trends form constraints on social interaction, but also enable that action in the first place and provide it with an identifiable shape. Within this field people pursue different strategies to attain or maintain gendered, ethnic, caste and religious identities. Personhood is also achieved, maintained and even deconstituted or reconfigured after death through these strategies. In pursuing different practices even the very composition and character of a person may change. In many communities not every human being is recognized as a person, or fully a person, or accorded the rights of other people. Categories of personhood are clearly dependent upon social relations, including in some contexts, tragically, factors like race or slavery. The attribution of personhood is therefore a vital area of archaeological study, alongside the attribution of gender, sexuality, ethnicity, class and caste. Nonetheless, overarching logics of personhood do exist, and should be a focus of archaeological enquiry. Without them, and the principles structuring their mobilization, it is difficult to frame the diverse social strategies people pursue. However, as we will see, these conditions and principles exist at a variety of scales, and not only affect individuals but communities conceptualized as a whole.

Moving up a scale: fractal personhood

So far we have examined different ways that individual human beings can be persons. However, it has already been mentioned in passing that in Melanesia a gift is a person, and a clan is a person. How is this possible? Just as people combine a diversity of relations, so clans combine a diversity of persons: the composite person exists in the same format at both scales. In this section we examine how the same kind of personhood can apply to individuals and to groups since the same relations compose them both.

Fractal personhood in Melanesia

Strathern argues that gatherings and ceremonies bring together a whole Highland New Guinea clan as a dividual person, so that '[t]he bringing together of many persons is just like the bringing together of one' (Strathern 1988: 14). The clan is also internally differentiated, and encompasses a series of distinct parts usually disparate from each other (including the people within it, but also pigs, shell goods, etc). In order to appear as a dividual entity the clan suppresses internal difference, and draws together all of its elements to achieve the unity of 'one' collective while also being multiply-constituted (Strathern 1988: 276, fig. 4, and 1991b: 213). Both clans and individuals therefore move between being one person with many relations (dividual), and being presented as one of a pair in a relationship (partible) (Strathern 1988: 15). Unlike the single person the clan is usually fragmented and partible, but becomes dividual during social gatherings. The clan and the person therefore have parallel compositions and move between parallel conditions of personhood:

> The condition of multiple constitution, the person composed of diverse relations, also makes the person a partible entity: an agent can dispose of parts, or act as a part.

Thus 'women' move in marriage as parts of clans; thus 'men' circulate objectified parts of themselves among themselves.

(Strathern 1988: 324–5)

So the clan is like a person: it is one form of the *collective* person (a family might be another). The clan, and each community within it is conceptualized as a whole person, and Strathern (1988: 260) details how male dancers move in unison as a group during a gathering, as though they were a single person. Here, physical comportment accentuates the equivalence of singular and collective personhood. There are also some categories of person who frequently act for the whole clan as both collective and singular persons. To take just one category of 'fractal' person as an example, many Highland New Guinea clans are presented as a person and embodied by a single person, a 'big man', during ceremonial exchanges (Godelier and Strathern 1991; Mosko 1992; Strathern 1991a, 1991b). These people are able to carry out particular types of exchanges and transformations on behalf of the community, drawing the community together. In Strathern's (1991b) rendition, big men present the clan as a person seen by outsiders. The social relations within the clan are produced equally within the big man. Big men are equivalent to each other person in the community (in our terms 'equal'), are composed out of the products of other people, and are a version of the clan as a whole. Rumsey (2000) reports that New Guinea Highland big men use the pronoun 'I' to refer to their group as a whole. Exchanges between big men are exchanges between clans: the clans are equivalent, and so are all persons within them, including the big man (Strathern 1991b: 200–1). In other words, the diagram Figure 2.1 applies equally to a single person and to a clan: it is the mechanism of gift exchanges. All people move between scales, scaling down the size of community they contain in jettisoning parts, and scaling up by forming new relations. Big men operate at both the scale of the individual and the community at once.

Roy Wagner (1991) refers to this phenomenon of equivalent personhood appearing at different scales as a *fractal* conception of person and world. The 'whole' of any single person's body is both part of a larger body (the clan) and also composed of smaller bodies which are themselves also internally complete (e.g. different blood-lines). Like a Mandlebrot set, the same pattern is repeated within itself but produces different forms. Each unit, each body, is therefore 'one' and 'many'; that is, one person composed of many relations, or one family with many persons, or one clan with many families, and so on. The clan is a person at a different scale, so the single person is a fractal equivalent of the clan (Gell 1999: 49). Even the universe or the natural world may be thought of as an entity equivalent to the human person (e.g. Gell 1999; Wagner 1991: 167). It is not just a clan that can be a fractal person – any collective entity like a family or house may be. And in societies with a fractal notion of the person, any single person is a fractal person too. Some people can, however, encapsulate greater scales than others or articulate changes of scale and acts of separation and re-articulation in different ways (Strathern 1991b; Mosko 1992; and see Box 3.2).

Fractal Hindu personhood

Fractals are also a feature of Hindu personhood (Wagner 1991: 172). There is no distinction between the different scales of body involved in social relations, so that each person contains the same substances as their caste, drawn from the cosmos. Special kinds of person can come to encapsulate the whole cosmos in their person. Some seek deliberately to combine the sacred and the impure, the most potent of all substance-codes. Ascetics and other holy figures may, for example, eat human waste or even bodily remains and engage in impure sexual congress (Parry 1982, and 1994: ch. 8). Their ability to do this marks them as able to transform the excessively gross and extremely subtle and create undifferentiated, primordial substance-code (Parry 1982). They encapsulate the cosmos as undifferentiated substance within them. An ascetic still lives in a fractal world, and the body of the person is a key node in all of these transactions. They operate at the scale of the one and the many, right up to the level of the cosmos. Oestigaard (in press) describes how the Nepalese king is the kingdom, and the incarnation of Vishnu on earth, and translates the caste system and all of the differently charged substances within that system into his body (cf. Marriott 1976). Disposing of the royal body is an act of cosmogony, something that re-orders and renews the world. Treating any single human body may have less to do with their individuality than to do with their place as a person who encapsulates a particular form of social relations at one scale among others. Their containment of particular essences may be of the utmost importance.

Fractals and representation

The range of scales that a fractal person may cover (i.e. whether they encapsulate a clan, a caste or the cosmos and the impact of their actions on each of these) may vary considerably depending upon the context of an event. Parts of a person, and people as parts of a community, may carry the same features as the whole. This throws up an archaeological challenge in recognizing parts in relation to wholes, discussed in later chapters. It also suggests an archaeological problem since we cannot reasonably expect all past people to be simply microcosms of a social order. All past people were not treated the same. However, while the kinds of relations operate at all scales, the strategies pursued through those relations may still be variable. Fractal personhood does not in itself restrict difference. Can we therefore understand western individuals as fractal? Not in our common conception of the world, since individuals cannot extract parts of themselves to give to others, and are not composed of essences that flow through the cosmos. Individuals are conceived of as impermeable to this world, and in the world of individuals people and things *represent* one thing or another; they are not integral to one thing or another (Chapman 2000: 32; Wagner 1991: 165). Fractal personhood, therefore, is only viable when communities and things as well as individuals can be thought of as persons who interpenetrate one another. This will become clearer through analysis of the role objects play in gift exchanges.

Conclusion

People themselves are multiply-authored, then, though the extent to which this is so is not always recognized in western culture. We should not expect that individuals' motivations and desires are always centred around individuality, and should not underestimate the impact of modes of personhood that place the emphasis elsewhere. Ethnographic analogies are a vital part of the search for past forms of personhood. The accounts presented here stand as comparatives enriching the archeological imagination (Thomas 1996: 63–4), and illustrate how personhood is generated through trends in social relations. People deploy differing strategies in negotiating personal identities for themselves and others through the larger trends in practice that structure their lives. Partibility and permeability are two such trends integral to the production of distinctive forms of personhood. Archaeologists can interpret personhood by looking for the mechanisms of transactions between people, and the strategies they employ through those mechanisms. Furthermore, since people are transformed by their interactions, evidence for personal transformations are also fundamental to archaeological investigations of personhood. Objects, animals and groups of people can also be understood as people, since they are constituted through the same processes, and we will see that they are often accorded self-determination and self-awareness in their attainment of personhood. Through fractal logic, groups of people may appear as one person, constituted through the same relations as single members of the community. This is only the beginning of how personhood can be accorded to beings other than individuals.

3

PERSONHOOD, EXCHANGE AND ARTEFACTS

Introduction

This chapter focuses on the role of material culture in articulating relations between people, exploring the role of artefacts in partible personhood as an example throughout. This chapter provides some examples of how objects mediate in relationships that join and separate people, showing how the little transactions of things between people convey personal qualities from one person to another. It also turns the spotlight on the contextual practices that throw people and objects into direct comparison, as well as those that temporarily distinguish them from one another. Finally, it assesses the potential for archaeological investigations of personhood afforded by patterns in the treatment of artefacts.

Gifts: objects as parts of people

Notions of ownership are as contextually specific as notions of personhood; in fact the two concepts are inextricable. Western individuality implies individual ownership of the indivisible human body. An individual can also own things, acquired from others or made by him or herself. However, this concept of ownership and production is not helpful in thinking about personhood outside modernity in many cases, since people are not always the individual owners of what we would see as their bodies, their work, their objects or land. A pig does not belong to a Hagen husband normally, but is the joint product of the domestic entity he belongs to: it is therefore more equivalent to him than owned by him. But, paradoxically, it *seems* to belong to him when he gives it away in ceremonial exchange (Strathern 1988: 148, 165). This is quite different to western ideas of individual ownership since it provides such a temporary position for both the man and the pig to occupy. A thing might belong to a social group, but not necessarily be owned by anyone as a private possession in our conception (Miller 1987: 121). In other words, a pig may share 'belonging' with human family members, not belong to them. Outside of capitalism gifts may be persons and may also be parts of persons. In order to unravel this close affinity between gifts and persons we turn to some research on gift exchange in Melanesia and Polynesia, where such connections are highly apparent. It would seem that in Indian personhood ties between people are substantial rather than mediated by distinct things that become objectified and personified (Busby 1997: 275). For that reason Indian exchanges and their effects are left to later chapters.

Exchange and gifts

Anything may be exchanged between people: opinions, stories or histories, blows, food, objects or even bodily substances. Each side of the exchange is usually separated by time (Mauss 1990: 35–6). Exchange is focused on the future, and when a person receives a gift they take on a debt. When they respond to the gift they in turn hold a debt over the recipient. In these exchanges each person changes perspective; they exchange social positions and power relations (Strathern 1996, and 1999: 99). The objects exchanged mediate those relations and become the markers of connections between people. Exchanges can also mediate relations between humans and non-human entities, or collective persons. Exchanges may take place between groups and families, and the item of exchange may include a person (e.g. Godelier 1999; Strathern 1988; Mauss 1990). Strathern (1992b) has stated that 'gift' and 'person' could be interchangeable terms in a Melanesian context. The object exchanged, as we have seen, may also be a person since it contains the kinds of relations and efficacy that persons encapsulate. More fundamentally, it is also a part of a person. Mauss argues that:

> to accept something from somebody is to accept some part of his spiritual essence, of his soul. To retain that thing would be dangerous and mortal, not only because it would be against law and morality, but also because that thing would be coming from the person not only morally, but physically and spiritually, that essence, that food, those goods . . . all exert a magical or religious hold over you.
>
> (Mauss 1990: 12)

For this reason gifts cannot ever really be kept or possessed, but are always in circulation. A gift is basically a part of a person or collective, or place, or any other entity that is given to another. To give a gift is to give a part of oneself:

> If one gives things and returns them, it is because one is giving and returning 'respects' . . . [y]et it is also because by giving one is also giving *oneself*, and if one gives oneself, it is because one 'owes' *oneself* – one's person and one's goods – to others.
>
> (Mauss 1990: 46)

In this sense the person is fully relational, and not owned by an individual, as in our conception, but owed by the self to others. This debt may be repaid with things, but is also repaid through effort, labour, time, words and substances – including human bodily substances. The circulation of substance-codes in India is vital to the generation and renewal of personhood, and the transmission of bodily substances is a key part of how persons are 'fed' or 'grown' in Melanesia. In both cases the very substances of the body are circulated throughout the community. However, the transmission of substances will be dealt with in Chapter 5; here we are concerned with artefacts as gifts, and the effect that inter-acting with such things has on personhood.

Objects mediate exchange

[T]he detachability of items has nothing to do with alienation: the parts circulate as parts of persons . . .

(Strathern 1988: 192)

If internal divisions in the Melanesian body make exter-nal objects seem parts of the person, the detachability of external objects gives a potential detachability and objectification to internal parts [of the person].

(Busby 1997: 275)

Strathern draws a distinction between mediated and unmediated exchange in Highland New Guinea (Strathern 1988: 178–207). Unmediated exchanges have no visible gifts, but involve the direct transmission of essences between bodies: these are discussed in Chapter 5. Mediated exchange involves a visible gift, and requires a process of partibility. For the purpose of this analysis we could think of a gift as a substitute or visible condensation of the blood from another family that must be extracted from the person and given to that family (Mosko 1992: 704). Mediated exchanges involve objects that are at once conceptualized as part of the person, and also extracted out of the person for exchange purposes. Mediated exchanges can be 'external' to a person, family, clan: in fact, they require that a part of the person which actually originates from that other clan is extracted and returned. The absence of this element of another's family in one's person would leave one free, for instance, to marry into that family. In other words, they involve externalization of some part of the person. The gift given is the part that is 'owed to others'. The part moving between people carries a debt with it, and a gift of this sort, like a cutting from a plant, can be used to start fresh relationships in new gardens. Once fully grown, the fruits of the gift will be returned – gift exchange is not reciprocal but cumulative. In effect, the gift is a part of both people carrying out the exchange, and forms an enduring debt which grows and is repaid, grows and is repaid, on either side until other events stop the exchange partnership. Giving a gift reduces the scale of the person temporarily, but allows – or rather demands – later replacement with a different 'return' gift object (see Figure 2.1). Mediated exchange is therefore the arena in which the dividual person is reduced, made partible, and reconfigured.

Gifts are inextricable from a relationship between donor and recipient: they are the fulcrums around which personal attachments pivot. Gifts that move between people like this are referred to as inalienable from the relationship between those people (Weiner 1992; Mosko 2000). However, return gifts will not be the same specific object as was received, so different individual objects will become inalienable from the same relationship. A distinction should therefore be made between a gift relationship and a gift object. So one gift object, like a pot, might be given from one woman to another. The other woman, some months later, may continue the gift relationship by giving a valuable ornament to the first woman. Each object is inalienable from the relationship while it is the hinge between the women: the ornament takes over from the pot. The most recent gift object frequently 'covers' older ones, freeing them up for further use in other relationships (e.g. Barraud et al. 1994: 53). Therefore owing and being owed a gift may tie people together and that tie may be manifested in an object, but over time several different objects will feature in the gift relationship. The old gift objects move on to new relationships (see Godelier 1999: 53–5; Mauss 1990: 14–16). This said, these gifts continue to circulate as gifts: the pot would be given by the second woman to yet another woman so that it w4 ould become inalienable from yet another relationship. Inalienable goods carry with them an intimate connection with each relationship they were part of: they retain a part of each person who has authored their history. Inalienable things may therefore carry biographies and have social identities: they are persons. However, inalienable things should be not be equated with individual people. They are dividual, conjoining many people. They may not be possessed: no gift object is inalienable from a single person. Inalienability is not ownership.

Gift-giving connects people, then, but it also separates people as well (Strathern 1988: ch. 8). Exchanging gifts allows people to exchange perspectives, to become the debtor and the creditor respectively (Strathern 1999: 239). The donor shrinks in scale and releases that part of them that is owed to another. A part of the person, whether a singular person or the community as a person, is presented as a visible gift. Crucially, this whole process is vital to social regeneration. Parts must be extracted and manipulated for there to be any possibility of change, renewal and creation among the whole (Gell 1999: 53). Breaking people apart, and separating them, is thus a vital process in the perpetuation of dividual and partible relationships and people. As we will see this has led to some pointers for archaeologists interested in partibility as a principle structuring personhood.

Commodities and the sacred

Gifts, being inalienable from people, and from the relations between them, are unlike commodities (Appadurai 1986; Godelier 1999; Miller 1987; Mosko 2000; Strathern 1988: 143–5). Commodities, like factory-made goods, can be divorced from their context of production and from their makers, and they are easily separated from those who sell them. They are not a part of any person at any scale. However, commodities do exist in non-capitalist societies, and the distinction between inalienable gifts and alienable commodities is not a rigid one. Commodities are also not entirely alienable. Even after it has been extricated from a factory and shop, a can of coke is still integral to a series of relationships and effects, such as maintaining the economy of the company that produced it. But it is not used to record any ongoing relationships and once consumed it is worthless, unless turned into a piece of art, for example. As an artwork the can of coke might become integral to a community, and can be consumed repeatedly as such. However, nobody is expected to give a return gift for the can of coke, or for viewing the artwork.

These have not been extracted from anyone to be absorbed by someone else: they can be paid for. The producers and consumers are integral individuals, and by paying for the can of coke the buyer has effectively bought out of any personal relationship with the vendor. Such relations may only be built by other exchanges, like conversations, for example. A different kind of object exists alongside a different concept of the person (see also Chapman 1996).

We could refer to things that are able to feed relations again and again, whose effects are consumed repeatedly, and that lie at the heart of a community's identity as sacred (Godelier 1999: 72, 111, 121–3, 164–6). Sacred things cannot normally be given away. Obviously, exactly what is sacred is a contextual matter. For example, it may be that even commodities are in some cases sacred; food, the dead, and even waste products may be involved in sacred cycles of fertility and reproduction (e.g. Bloch and Parry 1982; Moore 1986). We can see the very materials of the human body as sacred to some degree. How sacred qualities are transmitted will be discussed in the fifth chapter. Things can move between all three of these conditions in their biographies, being at one time commodities, at another gifts, and at others sacred (Appadurai 1986; Kopytoff 1986). From an archaeological point of view we can postulate that all *things* are potentially inalienable and alienable to some degree: while gift relations are the inalienable connections between two people, gift objects may in certain situations be extracted from one of these relationships and relocated to another. However, in a general sense, these things are inalienable objects in that they are not circulating as alienated objects distinct from persons: they are persons, and they are parts of persons.

Objects as people

It is only through activity that people in Melanesia appear as persons, through their ability to have a social effect on or in others. This is one reason why non-human things can be persons: because they have effects, and because they can be seen as active in social relationships. The pig exchanged by a Hagen man is a dividual, multiply-authored product of the household relations that produced it, and is then made into a partible object of exchange. But it is also a person (Strathern 1988: 200). Such items of exchange also illustrate a person's ability to produce gifts/persons and the ability to elicit gifts/persons from exchange partners in return (Gell 1999: 48). There is little to tell between people, animals and objects as gifts. In fractal personhood of this kind all products of multiple authorship may themselves contain the relationships necessary to make a person. They are therefore the equivalents of people. This section pursues a broad range of instances in which objects and animals may be recognized as people. It is difficult to know whether a past object was a thing, a person, or just *like* a person. However, we may be able to deduce its social effects, and how those are distributed through time and space. For this reason, while recognizing that objects may become persons, it may be more significant that objects can convey the same qualities as people, have the same effects as them, emerge from the same relations, and become encapsulated by them (and see Strathern 1999: 17). The centrality of objects in these relationships may go a long way to explaining why things may themselves become persons. Furthermore, the treatment of objects is as indicative of trends in personhood as the treatment of human bodies.

Battaglia (1990) describes how the Sabarl axe and limestick are personified, and their bodies attributed body parts like human beings. The axe stands as a metaphor for the whole person with its body parts correlating to human body parts – the blade as the hand or genitals, the shaft as an arm with an elbow (Figure 3.1; cf. Tilley 1996: 72–5). Each part is also named after a part of the clan, since the axe, as a clan member, consists of clan elements. The similarity between clan, people and axes is perhaps clearest in their containment of the quality *hinona*. Battaglia (1990: 40) describes *hinona* as the vital substance, life-force, productive potential or fertile quality of a person or thing. In this case it is the blade of the axe which is most associated with *hinona* – though for humans *hinona* is most frequently

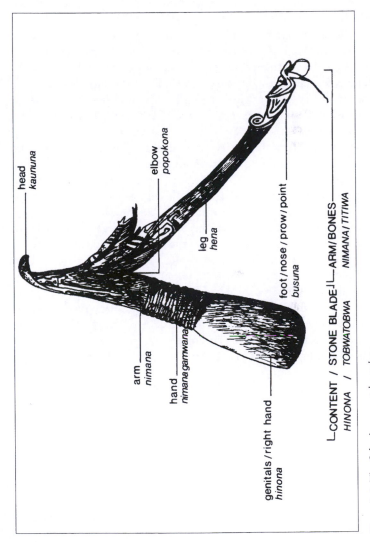

head
kaununa

elbow
popokona

leg
hena

arm
nimana

hand
nimanagamwana

foot/nose/prow/point
busuna

genitals/right hand
hinona

CONTENT / STONE BLADE / ARM/BONES
HINONA / TOBWATOBWA   NIMANA/TITIWA

Figure 3.1 The Sabarl axe or *tobwatobwa*.

Source: Reproduced from Battaglia (1990: fig. 9), with kind permission of Chicago University Press.

observed in the genitals or the right hand which guides exchange. Like a human body the axe gets 'hot' in action, a sign of *hinona*. *Hinona* can be harnessed in producing the person and also the object; gift and person exist in a relationship of mutual production (Battaglia 1990: 133–4). The Sabarl axe is also a material metaphor for exchange relations and the movement of gifts in mortuary exchanges, since the 'elbow' that articulates the axe also mirrors the shape of exchange relations (Battaglia 1990: 112, 134–5). Like a human body, the axe is evidence of relationships, of its own mobility and multiplicity, and of the mobility and generative potential of the owner and their kin. It participates in the same social action as other persons. A community of axes gather together in Sabarl mortuary rites, donated by relatives, and this clustering of axes along with food composes the 'corpse' of the deceased (Battaglia 1990: 177–8). The redistribution of this corpse is synonymous with the decomposition of the person, and the return of their components and relations to the wider community. This illustrates the Sabarl person as a dividual, and importance of axes both as people and as parts of people. In Sabarl society each axe is a gift, and it is like a person; it is an animate object, equivalent to a human person in the community.

Mauss (1990) cites the example of the Polynesian concept of the *hau* of a thing or creature to explain the animacy of non-human beings. The *hau* is the spirit of an object, which is in a way a kind of detached spirit of the place where the thing originated. For example, forest birds contain the *hau* of the forest, they are its *exuviae* and contain its generative potential or spiritual potency (Gell 1998: 106–8; Mauss 1990; Godelier 1999: 16–17, 49–56). The *hau* desires a return to its place of origin and the group and person who made it. When objects are exchanged the *hau* of the object moves with it, following the route of the thing and ensuring that it keeps moving until it can return home. Like people, things and places can share a quality something like a spirit. Like human bodies, things can be composed of a plurality of substances (stone, wood, resin), body parts (blade, shaft, elbow) and relations (to the land the tree was grown on, to axes from the same tree, to quarries, to the giver and receiver, etc.). Like persons with minds, souls and bodies (for instance), things can be composed of multiple qualities and convey the essences of living beings. Objects can be like persons because they exhibit the same qualities, including souls, the ability to move, to negotiate, to age and even die, and often desires, such as the desire to return home.

Box 3.1 Late Bronze Age swords in northern and central Europe: animate objects with personalities and destinies

Mike Williams (2001, 2002) has recently argued that later Bronze Age swords may have been seen as persons. Swords travelled great distances from central Europe into northern Europe, and were desirable exotic items. The life-cycle of northern European swords suggests they were objects with personalities and destinies (Williams 2002). Swords were smelted and crafted on river banks often a great distance from where the ores were procured. Rivers can be seen as places of transformation in European prehistory, frequently associated with transitions between life and death, and one world and another (Bradley 2000). Williams considers that in some cases these rivers may also have been political boundaries (cf. Bradley 2000: 159). The positioning of metalworking by rivers marks the practice as liminal as well as highly transformative, turning rock to liquid and then to metal. Drawing on African ethnographies, Williams argues that this smelting was a sexualised act, akin to human reproduction. At the end of their lives many exotic swords in northern Europe were frequently returned to rivers and other wetland locations, where they were violently broken and disposed of. In central Europe swords were instead buried in graves. In both cases Williams focuses on the sword itself as a dead person. He draws an analogy with Inuit shamanic practice in which the tools used to butcher and process polar bear

continued on next page

---

carcasses have souls. These items are offered to the skin of the bear, whose soul will not depart to the spirit world alone. In the central European burials we could imagine the person accompanied by another soul, while in the northern Europe context it seems that swords themselves were ritually killed and thrown into the entrances to the underworld. Burials were rare in parts of northern Europe during the later Bronze Age, and it may be that the bodies of the human dead were committed to the water along with their companion swords (Bradley 2000: 56). Furthermore, parallel violent treatment was often enacted on the dead deposited in watery locations in northern Europe in the Bronze and Iron Ages (Glob 1969; M. Williams 2003; Oestigaard 2000). Swords may indeed have been people, and an integral part of personhood in the late Bronze Age.

Archaeology, gifts and partible personhood

The inalienability of gifts from relationships between people has been a fruitful concept for archaeologists. In a world where people are partible gifts are parts of people, and, as persons, these gifts may themselves contain heterogeneous parts. In turn, therefore, objects may be rendered partial and their parts exchanged. Here we review some recent work by prehistorians which has built on the concept of inalienable things and dividual personhood, and also raise a few caveats.

Biography and inalienable objects

Archaeologists have taken to the feature of gifts as artefacts with a social biography and even personality (e.g. Jones 2002b: 83–167; Thomas 1996: ch. 6; Tilley 1996: ch. 6). These studies show that the biographies of particular artefacts, and of classes of artefact, are far from transparent. Biography is not simply acquired in an accumulative fashion. The histories associated with any object may change over time (Jones 2002b: 102). Indeed, objects are not inalienable from their history so much as the relationships they currently mediate. A gift *object* can therefore be extracted from one relationship and made inalienable from another – for example, through a chain of exchange relations extending over a long distance which may sever an artefact from the knowledge about its real source and production (Chapman 1996: 209, and 2000: 32). In some cases this may involve revising stories about their past. For this reason biographical approaches are most effective when they locate the contextual significance of the object at particular stages in its biography. Biographical approaches are only effective when the whole story is considered, from the extraction of natural substances, to the conception and construction of the object, through various stages of use and modification, repeated acts of consumption, destruction, and the use of the fragmented components (Jones 2002b: ch. 5). Throughout this book it is argued that the same is true of people in the past, and that such transformations are integral to personhood.

Artefacts, like people, are multiply-authored, and archaeologists cannot be sure that all of the stages in object production were carried out by one individual or that all components of an object were produced by one individual (Finlay 2003). A copper axe may create a chain of relations between the copper miner, the smelter, the finisher, and exchange partners. Each of these people may have been distributed along a caste-structure or similar arrangement of labour. Each time a gift is given, so parts of people are removed and exchanged, so that some people come to hold the parts of others. Gift objects themselves move further and further afield, and pass through being a part of many different people. The gift here, like the person, is also not an individual, but a dividual which exchanges one part of itself for another (i.e., in our eyes, one owner for another). In a world where personhood is dividual and fractal, then so are any objects inalienable from human relationships.

Partibility and fragmentation

One of the key elements of partibility is separation: the fragmentation of people and redistribution of their parts. One of the most sophisticated and extensive studies of personhood in European prehistory is presented by Chapman (2000) in one of a series of publications examining the articulation of parts and wholes in the Balkan Mesolithic, Neolithic and Chalcolithic periods (see also Chapman 1996 in particular). Chapman uses two concepts to describe two ways that objects mediate relations between people: enchainment and accumulation. Enchainment describes relations between people generated through the giving and receiving of inalienable objects. The chain describes the way that an object connects people along its path between different exchange partners. Chapman argues that both fragments of things (e.g. limbs broken from figurines, potsherds) and whole things can be used in enchained relations (2000: 37, 39). Accumulation, on the other hand, describes the collection of groups or sets of whole things by various social agents. Initially, such collections acted to integrate the community, and could be seen as a form of enchainment (Chapman 2000: 45, 47): we can perhaps imagine early 'hoards' as lain down during communal gatherings that celebrated joint membership of the collective person. However, Chapman argues, over time the accumulation of intact objects or the components for making them was appropriated by sub-groups of the community or powerful individuals. 'With accumulation, the value of the object or sets of objects became more significant than the relation of circulation' (Chapman 2000: 47). While both whole and fractured artefacts may become media for enchainment, accumulation thrives on intact things. Metalworking, and cast copper and gold in particular, allowed the production of sets of things which could be accumulated. Taking a dialectic approach to these two trends, Chapman postulates that enchained relations were gradually replaced over the millennia by relations of accumulation (Chapman 2000: 47). Relatively equal kin relations, maintained since the later Mesolithic, gradually gave way to the emergence of wealthy groups and individuals in the climax Copper Age (Chapman 2000: 47–8). Chapman's thesis is that long-distance exchange items found in hoards indicate growing accumulations of alienable wealth, not integrated in local productive relationships. However, vitally, he recognises these patterns as ideological presentations, claims and counter-claims made by past agents, not reflections of reality (2000: 130–1): they are *strategies* within a general logic of relations as perceived by prehistoric social agents. Yet tensions between claimants ultimately had a disintegrating effect on social relations, leading to social inequalities and the fragmentation of traditional communities.

It is enchainment which interests me here. I would like to compare the view of Melanesian gift exchange presented above with Chapman's interpretation of enchainment in Balkan prehistory. Melanesian gift objects support enchainment since they are parts of people which can be passed on indefinitely. These objects cannot be held by two people at once. Dividing and sharing the fragments of things, like sherds from broken pots and figurines, may allow for people to share a part of the *same* thing at the *same* time. There are, then, potentially some key differences between the enchained relations that Chapman identifies as operating through these fragmented things and Melanesian gift exchanges. First, objects like shell goods in Melanesia acquire additional parts as they move; they are not fragmented. As Chapman (2000: 6) acknowledges, fragmented things have a finite range of movement since they cannot be halved indefinitely. *Kula* objects are more likely to grow in size and repute as they encapsulate more and more relations. This leads to the question of the value of a fragment in Chapman's scheme: was it also a whole object which could circulate as a thing with its own value? Chapman's analogies are initially with halved objects which are 'tokens' of relationships, like medieval indentured charters two halves of which were to be brought together in commemoration of an original agreement over property (Chapman 2000: 6, 37–8, 86). Yet as Chapman acknowledges (2000: 39), medieval indentured charters is perhaps an unfortunate analogy, and instead he pursues the angle that the prehistoric fragmented things were inalienable from relationships formed during the event in which the whole object was broken. It would seem, then, that fragments were not tokens standing for alienable property: in fractal relations things and people extend out of other things and people, while in representational thinking things and people stand for one another (Chapman 2000: 32). Therefore fragmented yet inalienable things would not be tokens, but parts of people or communities. There is nothing to prevent potsherds or figurine fragments being exchanged like Melanesian shell goods, then, though it may be difficult for us to see what effects such objects might have. Shell goods are dazzling, complex and luminous, for instance, and can be exchanged for pigs. While such a role can be identified for shell goods in the Neolithic (Chapman 2000: 99), it is unclear how potsherds might operate in a similar way, although it may be that they held some essential quality that made them of value. Either a substantial or historic quality (e.g. a commemorative role; Chapman 2000: 227), or both, might be implied, particularly in cases when fragmented items are curated over long periods of time. It is only if there was some substantial or objectified value to the potsherds that they could operate through asymmetrical exchange relations to chain partible people together; otherwise the kind of enchainment involved might be rather different to that of exchange items. Gifts of whole objects in Melanesia separate people but also require a return gift, linking them together in a relationship that is never equal: each partner is always alternating positions with the other (debtor/creditor). It is therefore also necessary to know whether a fragment was exchanged as an object in its own right, or whether what was taken away from something like a pot-smashing episode was an equal share among all parties concerned. In other words, there is a difference between whole or fragmented objects being exchanged along lines of relationships, and a situation where each fragment of a thing stays with those who participated in an event involving its fragmentation, and the fragment acts as a memento of that event. To use an analogy to explain such sharing of equal things, Kirtsoglou describes the phenomenon of 'bonded' objects; a pair of objects like watches or lighters worn by two lovers citing a link between them (Kirtsoglou 2002). Each single object is one identical half of a partnership; in this case a same-sex relationship. The donor gives one object to their partner, but keeps the other. As well as fragmented objects, two or more intact objects made from the same antler, bone or flint nodule might, for example, be bonded through shared origin. Bonding through holding identical objects or fragments of the same parent object simultaneously may be rather different to the relation of debt achieved in ongoing Melanesian partible exchanges. The link connects rather than separates, and would seem to imply a shared perspective rather than an exchange of perspectives. Perhaps fragmented things were vehicles for memory that formed a tie to the past, and denoted a shared perspective. Giving one half of a seal and keeping the other (Chapman 2000: 86–9, 227) might be interpreted as a statement of inclusion, perhaps running alongside other exchange relations that separated people and differentiated perspectives. Chapman (2000: 226) notes that there are many different ways that enchainment may operate in forming ties between people, and also that a tension exists between enchainment and accumulation. This is a most useful approach, then. First, it allows for consideration of different kinds of enchainments. And second it allows for exchange items to be both wealth and inalienable to some degree, and provides an archaeological framework for investigating mechanisms that mediated this relationship. To me some of Chapman's findings suggest that personhood in the Balkan Mesolithic, Neolithic and Copper Age operated through some quite different principles of partibility than ethnographies suggest of Melanesia. Indeed, one of the great strengths of Chapman's account is that it reveals technologies of personhood that are quite specific to the archaeological context under study. For example, Hamangia figurines might portray a female body while whole, but male genitalia when viewed in a certain way and when broken (Chapman 2000, 1996; cf. Knapp and Meskell 1997). Here it is snapping of limbs and heads from figurines that change their gender

(Chapman 2000: 74–6, and 2002a): partibility is effected literally by removing body parts. Chapman's study shows up yet other ways that the social practices can give shape to personhood, in a rich analysis of how the tension between partibility and indivisibility was mediated through material things and the bodies of the dead. If potsherds and other fragmented goods were accorded social value, as relics of past events and/or as meaningful substances or objects in their own right, then their place in chains of relations is of vital importance to archaeological research (see also Woodward 2002; Bradley 2000: 127–31; and Box 2.3).

Fragmentation is not in itself necessary for partible exchange relations, and forms of dividuality exist which do not require partibility at all, as Busby (1997) has demonstrated. Nonetheless, it remains as a good indicator of dividual personhood for archaeologists. The need to separate out elements of the world and redirect them in renewing the social world is a core theme in dividual personhood, and as we will see in the next two chapters the deconstitution of the person is a vital part of that process. The transmission of substances and essences can play a larger part in our interpretations of prehistoric relationships that redistribute parts of people and objects. However, this requires thinking of animals and objects not just as the objectified parts of people, but also persons in their own right. The redistribution of their broken bodies may have deconstituted them as people, allowing the circulation of important qualities associated with personhood.

Composite objects and the reintegration of parts

It is worth while to make a distinction at this point between fragments that are not wholes, and not used to produce composite objects (such as figurine limbs or potsherds), and those that are (such as the crafted fragments of *spondylus* shells that were turned into ornaments and exchanged across Neolithic Europe). For example, Jones points out that beads can be detached from early Bronze Age necklaces, while other beads can be added

(Jones 2002a). Each necklace is therefore a composite artefact through which chains of relations can be traced (see Chapter 6). Each bead is a complete object in itself and part of a larger whole: as an exchangeable part that can be repeatedly incorporated into a greater whole it is an excellent fractal object. Composite artefacts may also be multiply-authored. As Finlay (2003) suggests, many people could be linked together in producing a tool with multiple microlithic teeth, for instance. Composite objects, like sets of things temporarily drawn together, may be used to trace and change many relations and need not necessarily be seen as accumulations of wealth (cf. Chapman 2000: 108–12, 129–31). Sets of objects like those deposited in hoards might also be statements of community and social integration rather than the appropriation of wealth. Practices like hoarding and depositing rich burials need not have involved a movement towards increased alienability so much as disparate trends that reconfigured new sets of dividual relations. People who attract wealth in Melanesia, like big men or great men (or women for that matter: Battaglia 1991), are not indivisible individuals exercising alienating relations; they are fractal and partible mediators of exchange (Wagner 1991; Strathern 1991b; Mosko 1992). Ambiguity remains over when collections of things should be seen as the media of integrating acts drawing together a community or acts of appropriation by a subgroup or individual (see Box 3.2). While there will always be ambiguity over what can be thought of as a part or a whole, and when each might emerge as such, composite items and collections of items may all be useful places to start in examining dividual relations and fractal personhood in prehistory. Acts of separation and reintegration are likely to have been key features in any process of dividual relations.

Box 3.2 Gifts and the dead in later neolithic and early Bronze Age southern Britain

Rich graves from the late Neolithic and early Bronze Age in Wessex are frequently seen as containing the remains of those who controlled the distribution of prestigious goods and labour, the products of others. These intact bodies might seem to us like indivisible individuals of high status, and as evidence for increasing individual autonomy following periods when the dead were buried collectively or not at all (e.g. Clarke *et al.* 1985). However, there are other interpretations. In the earlier Neolithic human bones had been stored in chambered tombs, visited and circulated as artefacts of some value (Barrett 1988b; Lucas 1996; Thomas 2000a, 2002; and Chapter 5). Such trends in the fragmentation and circulation of the dead may have continued in a slightly different vein in the later Neolithic and early Bronze Age with the deliberate destruction of personal ornaments in the mortuary sphere (e.g. a well-worn wrist-guard at Hemp Knoll: H. Williams 2001; and another at Barnack: Last 1998: 45) and the circulation of some personal artefacts over generations. Woodward (2002) suggests that at least two kinds of fragmentary things – amber spacer beads from necklaces and sherds from broken Beaker vessels – were curated and circulated in the early Bronze Age (see also Bradley 2002: 57–8). Jones (2002a: 168) notes that 47 per cent of beads found in southern British graves were in groups of five beads or less, and were possibly just fragments of necklaces. While the dead may seem individuated in single burials the 'corpse' was frequently composed of many different materials and parts, including spectacular gold objects and necklaces of beads made from exotic materials (Jones 2002a: 168). The complexity and variety of things attached to the body attested to a multitude of relationships (Jones 2002a; Thomas 1991; Last 1998).

continued on facing page

Some of these people were cremated, others buried. Cremation deposits seldom contain all of the bones of the dead (McKinley 1997: 130), and the flesh was visibly relocated through immolation. Barrett (1994: 121) notes that many of the artefacts lain down with cremations had not been through the pyre, but added later. Arguably, the whole mortuary deposit could be seen as a gift (see also Lucas 1996: 114–15), donated by the community, and we could also see the deposition of bodies as gifts to supernatural forces (see Chapter 5). If we think of grave goods as gifts, then intact objects might be seen as impressive gifts. Such intact gifts are frequently intended to elicit a response, and so may connect the living and the dead. Equally, we might suggest that breaking an object or splitting a necklace indicates that a complete gift has not been given to the dead: they have no need to reciprocate. While keeping part of the necklace provides a vehicle for memory that stays among the living (Jones 2002a: 169), both strategies conjoin the living and the dead as well as separating them. As Jones (ibid.) also points out, the gathering of many objects in the graves could be seen as a feature of social integration, tracing many close ties between people (including, as we will see, past people) rather than the hoarding of wealth by powerful individuals. Cremations and burials could still be seen as transformative events, which brought together and 'finished' a person temporarily before personal components and essences were redistributed. This redistribution might involve the searing away of flesh, and/or the relocation of gifts in a cycle of mortuary feasts. The resultant deposit could be seen as the creation of the ancestral dead rather than a reflection of the individual identity of the deceased (Thomas 2000a).

The inclusion of artefacts in early Bronze Age graves has frequently been referred to as a kind of text we can read: these depositional practices have a grammar (Thomas 1991).

continued on next page

Daggers are common early Bronze Age grave goods, and many may also have been of some antiquity when buried (Bradley 2002: 55). The provision of daggers with some of the dead may mark them as people who cut, or separate out, parts of society for redistribution and cut and share out meat at feasts. Alternatively the daggers might have been left by whoever was responsible for those events, and for the burial. Daggers might signal that the dead were cut from the living. We could speculate a parallel in the cutting of the umbilical cord and the cutting away of the dead. Daggers were seldom worn by corpses in Yorkshire, but were rather placed in the graves under or alongside bodies or in hands (Lucas 1996: 113), and Barrett (1994: 117–19) suggests similar dedicatory acts in Wessex. Circulation of substances through consumption was also referenced through the inclusion of beakers and other vessels. Finally, the technology of cremation – itself a redistribution of personal substance into the cosmos – was perhaps referenced through inclusion of 'fire-making' paraphernalia in some graves (Lucas 1996: 114). The transformative potential of fire is again intelligible in the context of feasting. Among Melanesian societies 'big men' are those who integrate the entire community for exchanges with another group, while 'great men' separate out distinct components of the community for redistribution and mediate internal differences (Mosko 1992). Great men, a sub-community of the clan different in kind to other members, may take several heterogeneous forms, including sorcerers and warriors. While burials from this period are diverse, there was certainly a restricted range of ways to lay out the dead (see Last 1998; Thomas 1991). The burial of a fraction of society in the late neolithic and early Bronze Age might relate to heterogeneous social roles and types of person: differences between the strategies people pursued or the exchange roles they performed might have informed mourners' decisions to bury or cremate first,

continued on facing page

to raise a mound or not, what to deposit, and to deposit fractions of a thing or the whole. While there are different chronological (see Mizoguchi 1993) and regional patterns to be teased out here, different strategies for operating exchanges and transformations may be apparent through analysis of the mortuary sphere. Each of these acts afforded commemoration and separation together, but in differing ways (see H. Williams 2001). Ultimately, however, the mortuary process was part of a community strategy. The exact mechanisms of separation and reintegration might have taken a variety of forms, whether mediated by ritual specialists or not. Repeated patterns in the diversity of fractal relations seems a useful analogy.

There are two main points here. First, single graves should not be seen as representations of indivisible individuals, nor biographical statements of individuality (Thomas 1999a: 156). What counts as a whole or a part is a contextual matter: the body is a part of society, it contains the parts of many other people, each of whom might suffer its loss, and the constituent elements of the cosmos. The same is true of artefacts that may be parts of people. Second, where people and gifts are interchangeable to some degree, bodies and objects do not belong to an individual but the community. Fragments of a body need not commemorate individuals; the same is true for relic remains of old objects, which may be inalienable from the community and offered to the dead. Henges and the edges of barrows were key foci for the use and deposition of already ancient objects, during activities that we could argue contacted the dead and the past (Woodward 2002). Where beaker sherds were curated, these might be equated with a fragmented person, who had once been a permeable vessel. Knowledge of precisely *which* individual had held that vessel might be unimportant, however, and sherds may have been pulled from the middens of communal activities (Woodward 2002: 1041). These relic fragments

continued on next page

were then deposited during activities at henges like Mount Pleasant (Bradley 2000: 127–31). Exchange relations, including ceremonial exchanges and feasts held at henges, were perhaps monitored by all members of the community, including the dead: the politics of separating, giving and consuming were community concerns. We could argue that early Bronze Age partible people encapsulated many relations, and that the dead were still heavily cemented in ongoing social relations. Elements of the recent dead were frequently extracted back into the community, or perhaps given inalienable objects in expectation of return gifts. Whereas in the earlier Neolithic bodies had been fragmented and redistributed, here relations were traced through the circulation of relics, heirlooms or mementos (Barrett 1994: 122; Chapman 2000). Parts of the dead, or the past, were extracted into the community. The fragments of the distant dead were maintained in the community, and these too were sometimes given back through depositional practices. Personhood, then, was just as dividual in the later Neolithic and early Bronze Age as in the earlier Neolithic, then, but in different ways. Tensions between partible, permeable and individual characteristics of the person were reconfigured over the long term, but also throughout the biography of each person from conception and birth through to death and ancestry.

Interpreting personhood from material statements: ambiguous relations

Material remains are not the record of past activity but the media of past interactions (Barrett 1988a, 2001), and those interactions would have been ambiguous. Past bodies and objects were and are ambiguous sites for the production of meaning, and for making statements that might be contested (e.g. Thomas 1991; Tilley 1989, 1990; Yates and Nordbladh 1990; Yates 1993). All symbols are polyvalent, have multiple layers of meaning, and could be the focus of many divergent connotations to different people. People with conflicting interests may employ similar exchange strategies, similar forms of tracing relations. On the other hand, strategies in pursuing relations do often mark out groups with shared identities. Marriott outlines one logic to Hindu transactions, but many social strategies for engaging with that logic, strategies that cut as deeply as what to eat, when to speak, and how many words to use. The aspiration of Hindu personhood is the attainment of 'power understood as vital energy, substance-code of subtle, homogeneous quality, and high, consistent transactional status or rank' (Marriott 1976: 137). However, attempts to attain this state follow many paths, each of which involves careful monitoring of interactions and the refinement of one substance-code into another by exchanges. Furthermore, as Butler (1993) has shown, parody and subversive use of dominant practices may be very effective modes of engaging with, yet undermining, a particular activity. Meaning, and the pinning down of any identity, is ultimately endlessly deferred so that there is never any definitive closure (Derrida 1986; and see Russell in press). Since there would have been conflicts and contradictions within any context, there is unlikely to be any single interpretation of the successful negotiation of personhood; there are, rather, strategies for coping with the predominant field. Circulating parts and wholes are open to endless reinterpretation and reconfiguration in both orthodox and heterodox ways. So, what is part and what is whole may be endlessly reconfigured through different social events without *necessarily* leaving a visible trace on the object itself. Contextual activities temporarily gave objects identities as parts of one person rather than other, and as alienated things or dividual persons. Detailed contextual analyses like Chapman's (2000) are the surest way to build frames for interpreting these identities.

Conclusion

While capitalism produces a predominantly alienated form of exchange and a narrative of predominantly alienated and indivisible personhood, other cultural milieux generate rather different relations between human beings and things. In partible relations things can be persons, can be wealth, can be commodities: they may be wealth objects and inalienable things at the same time. In fractal thinking things can be parts of persons, and they can also be persons. While much can be done to examine the nature of personhood through archaeological remains, plural processes and interpretations of ambiguous material relations are still to be expected. However, things and people participate in 'the same semantic universe' (Howell 1989: 422) making a true distinction between them impossible. In the next chapter we return to the human body, and trace how dividual people become completely fragmented after death.

4

PERSONHOOD, DEATH AND TRANSFORMATION

To be in one state of personhood is always to potentially be in another. This chapter is concerned with ritualized transformations of the person, primarily through death and mortuary practices. This is crucial to the interpretation of personhood in the past both because we often have an abundance of information about mortuary practice and because death is one of the most dramatic transformations enacted on the person. We will see how persons are altered by death, changed into entities of a different kind, and impacted by the death of others. The discussion will revolve around death and the recently deceased, leaving considerations of the long dead to the next chapter. We will also see that death allows the accentuated transmission of personal qualities throughout society and the cosmos. Once again, examples of death in societies that stress relational personhood will be provided by discussion of Melanesian and Indian ethnographies. Death is both a part of life, and sees a radical shift in the personhood of the deceased and those they leave behind. It is demonstrated here that personhood can be interpreted on the basis of how the dead were treated in ways other than by tracing individual biographies. In doing so this chapter addresses the place of death and the dead in society.

The ritual process

Rites of passage are sacred arenas in which the person passes from one set of relations to another. These delimit dramatic changes in personal identity due to a shift in relations with other persons. Examples include: acceptance into society following birth (and sometimes after several years of early childhood); commencement of puberty, sexual relations, or other stages of adulthood (e.g. on the conception of a child where adulthood is coterminous with parenthood); marriage; passing from adulthood to mature adulthood and old age; and a variety of rites associated with stages of death, bereavement, the removal of widowhood/widowerhood, and the continuing movement of the dead through further changes. Arnold van Gennep (1960) identified three phases to rites of passage: the affirmation of existing social status and separation from that status; the liminal (or in-between) period of separation from the majority of society and social norms during which identities are reconfigured; and the reintegration of the person into society where their new status is acknowledged. Each rite employs this structure, according to both Turner (1969) and van Gennep. The symbols involved and the rite itself are fundamentally polyvalent and ambiguous, referring to wider contexts and commenting on the naturalized order of things (Turner 1967: 48–58). Their use sheds new light on the places of, for example, animals, objects and substances in the natural order, and comments on the meaning of relations with those things. Mortuary rites follow the same pattern as any other rite. It is common that the dead become ghosts, and eventually become ancestral spirits through future post-funerary mortuary rites, so it is not the case that the first mortuary ritual is their final rite of passage. However, all rites of passage often draw on reference to death and rebirth in that they apply the same structure as the mortuary rites: the removal of one identity and emergence of another. Meaning at one rite is transferred to others, using the same principles to structure experience of all features of the cosmos, all frames of personal identity. Rites often entail eating or fasting, ritualized movement, and painting, dressing, marking or even permanently altering the body through, for example, scarification. These are all transformative acts. The liminal phase of rites of passage often employ frightening, shocking and therefore highly memorable events which leave an impact on the body and the psyche (Fowler 1997; M. Williams 2003; Lewis 1980). Rites of passage, particularly initiation rites, are communal affairs that synchronize the experience of many members of an age group, for example, co-ordinating social identity. Other rites of passage like marriages and mortuary rites bring together a community and transform relations within it. Personhood is monitored and regulated through these events as much as through everyday practice, and we have taken this entrée to illustrate how identity is a community affair in which public performances play a vital part. Death and the treatment of the dead should be placed in this context, though this does not mean they can be reduced to simply symbolic acts or self-replicating social technologies.

Just like other rites, those associated with the dead may not be aimed at removing them from society, as we might expect, but at *reintegrating* them into society as different kinds of entities, different orders of person. Mortuary actions refer back to everyday practices that mould bodies, and reflect on personhood through the medium of a body that now has the potential to be *entirely* dismembered or dispersed. They often reverse the conception of the person. The mortuary sphere is focal in the movement of personal substance, the renegotiation of value, and transformation of personal identity among survivors as well as the deceased. Mortuary practices therefore have multiple roles, including the deconstitution of the person, and their reclassification as spirits, ghosts, ancestors, and other subsets of the community. While the dead are transformed persons, they are often present among the community either as identifiable forces, or through the recycling of their elements. Mortuary practice is only intelligible within the context of other social activity and general patterns in personhood, so that the death of a western individual is intelligible in a different way to the death of a Melanesian individual. While both are dead, and their loss will be mourned, both death and mourning take different forms and generate different kinds of people among the wider community through different relationships with the deceased.

Mortuary practice and the transformation of the person

The conception and constitution of the person is vital to under-standing deconstitution after death, and vice versa (Bloch 1989: 15), since death marks a gross change in the facets of personhood that might be brought to the fore (e.g. the extent of dividuality, individuality, partibility, etc.). This highlights the contextual nature of these tensions, as they shift throughout life and during and after death. Mortuary practices often deconstitute the person through production of their death, sometimes over very long periods of time. Components of the person are reconfigured. The spiritual and physical aspects of the person are either removed from society or redistributed among society and/or the cosmos, depending on the predominant mode of personhood. The exact nature of this process of deconstitution varies considerably and does not always revolve around the body of the deceased. This section starts with a discussion of the death and deconstitution of individuals in modern Britain and then considers the death of Melanesian dividual/partible and Indian permeable people as con-trasting examples of personhood.

The death of the modern individual: a historical perspective

> Good frend, for Jesus sake forbeare
> To digg the dust encloased heare.
> Bleste be ye man [that]y spares thes stones
> And curst be he [that]y moves my bones.
> William Shakespeare's tombstone

Just as the living person is subject to certain metaphors in western history, so too is the dead person. During the medieval period it was expected that the body would decay after death, and this corruption was displayed openly in stained glass windows, on sepulchres and on tombstones. The corruption of the body was to be expected, and the soul would move on to Heaven. This passage was often gradual, with the soul spending long periods of time in purgatory, sometimes remaining there forever. The living would say prayers for the dead to atone for their sins and speed their journey. Sarah Tarlow (2002) has demonstrated how this set of metaphors was replaced in the eighteenth and nineteenth centuries by metaphors of sleep and eternal rest. Skulls and crossed bones, and other motifs of corruption, were replaced by urns and vines, plants or flowers (see Deetz 1977). Victorians made 'death masks' to preserve the faces of the dead, took photographs of dressed corpses, and made bracelets and necklaces from human hair in order to maintain images of the deceased. The corruption of the body was carefully hidden during a period when the individual person was rapidly becoming the most basic and most important social phenomenon. This trend continued throughout the twentieth century with ever more focus on the maintenance of the youthful body under full control of individual will, and the avoidance of its corruption.

The death of modern western individuals can be characterized in the following way:

1 The dead are institutionalized (Mitford 1998; Barley 1995), treated by coroners and undertakers rather than their families. The bodies of the dead do not rest at home but are sequestered in morgues and cemeteries. This has the effect of removing death from the sphere of daily experience for people, unless it is their professional task to deal with the dying and the dead (Shilling 1993: 188–90). Death itself increasingly occurs in hospitals and similar institutions (Barley 1995).

2 The moment of death is controlled and recorded with pinpoint accuracy. While there are various medical definitions of how and when death occurs, death is itself a momentary event. Maurice Bloch (1989) argues that the 'sudden' death of western individuals relates precisely to their individuality and indivisibility: while alive individuals are linked together but internally monadic, but when dead some part (individuality?) has departed the body, leaving nothing but an empty shell.

3   The corruption of the body is always to be avoided. There are
    two techniques for ensuring this: cremation and single burial
    in a coffin.
4   It is the prevalent public image that the body is buried intact
    and whole. Cases when it is perceived that the whole body has
    not been cremated or buried can cause distress to relatives. In
    reality, some bodies are not buried or cremated whole due to
    organ donation.
5   The cremated remains are sometimes dispersed into the world,
    often in a location favoured by the deceased. Inhumed remains
    are removed from view. Both strategies negate any sign of
    decay. However, the dispersal of cremated remains is seen as
    releasing the soul, spirit, or another undefined feature of indi-
    viduality into the world or an afterlife.

Despite these observations, we could still argue that the modern
person is ultimately deconstituted through funerary rites and
the series of exchanges which accompany and follow these, not
in a single momentary event of death. While institutions inter-
vene in the event of death and the disposal of the body, the
social activity of mourning and coping with death is still managed
by family and friends.

In the 'Are'are mortuary rite the survivors bring together all of
the different components of the deceased person around the corpse
(e.g. pigs, taro, shell wealth), and present them as gifts (Barraud
et al. 1994; de Coppet 1981). Arguably, this act brings the ordi-
narily distributed person together in one place, at one time. While
alive the person is distributed throughout the material world, and
only becomes a completed person *temporarily* during this mortuary
rite. In this act all of the relationships that sustained and composed the person are brought together and made explicit in
material form. These goods are then divided up again and redistributed back among the living – the deceased person is broken
up and their elements dispersed both into the world and throughout society. This process of deconstituting the person after death is
a key part of the system of change and exchange among the living.

Over the years following the mortuary rite, a whole sequence of feasts and exchanges takes place as new relationships are negotiated, and the deceased is both forgotten and remembered as their goods become core to the identity of other people.

Arguably, a parallel phenomenon takes place following the death of a western individual. During a funeral the relatives and friends of the deceased gather together to commemorate and finish them as an individual. The person is deconstituted gradually over time through a series of processes which both remember and forget them. This might include displaying and circulating their photographs or accounts of their lives, family photos they had collected, or the redistribution of heirlooms or other intimate possessions and mementos among surviving relatives and friends. These things become inalienable from relations within the family, and come to presence the dead in the world of the living. They are the media through which the person is both remembered and forgotten. In both the 'Are'are ethnography and the modern British case the person is deconstituted through the reallocation of material culture and the construction of relationships among the living which may *seem* to bypass the deceased. The person is never fully removed from society, as the legacy of their genes and/or their human relationships endure through their surviving relatives, friends and associates. Material traces of their lives ensure that memories of them are conveyed onwards after their death. The body itself is somewhat displaced from this process, and is removed from consideration at the earliest opportunity. In a sense, the most distinctively individualistic feature of the person, the body, is passed out of society, while the other fragments of personal identity are circulated and redistributed. Mortuary practices dissipate the person, though the degree to which and the rate at which this occurs is contextually specific. In both cases here dividuation is increased following the particularization of the person at the funeral and their separation from the living (it should be noted, though, that the mourners are collectivized). There are, however, differences in how this is achieved through alternative social technologies, and these pertain to cultural differences in personhood. Historic ethnographies indicate that the excision of the corpse from redistribution is a recent development in Melanesia resulting from colonial contact, and that the body was frequently exhumed or disarticulated in the past (e.g. Hirsch 1990: 27; Maschio 1994: 92–3; Strathern 1982: 117). The social effects of a western funeral followed by *ad hoc* acts of remembrance (e.g. looking at photo albums) contrast with the Melanesian ritualized cycle of memorial exchanges that may continue for many years. Different materialities and tempos are produced in each case. It is also notable that death itself is never 'natural' in Melanesia or India. Like the conception of a person, death must be brought about by social agency: in Melanesia frequently through sorcery, in India through the 'killing' of the corpse. Furthermore, the process of death only slowly separates people from their things and bodies: the parts left behind are not worthless, but highly valued (Bloch 1989). They are owed to the community, and must be returned to the forces in the cosmos that donated them in the first place. The emergence of specific people as named and powerful ancestors after their death is the presentation of one aspect of the person as the whole. Elevation to this status requires the removal of other components of that person and sometimes lengthy periods of investment in aggrandizing the deceased by descendants. The production of ancestors is dependent on the living (e.g. Watson 1982: 156).

In many prehistoric European communities human bodies or their parts or substances were circulated, curated and deposited alongside animal bones, natural materials and artefacts. In societies that left bodies in accessible Neolithic chambers and removed the bones, left their dead to decay in the open, or cremated their dead and distributed the remains, the dividuality of the person was made apparent by treatment of the dead body (Fowler 2001, 2003). Before discussing this case briefly I turn to the death of the person and the relocation of dividual personal aspects like the soul or the spirit.

Death and the transformation of the aspects of the person: the fate of dividual and partible persons

> The first part of the funeral ritual comes to an end with the burial of the corpse, whose humours are said to turn into pigs and other forest animals.
> (Barraud *et al.* 1994: 36, describing an Orokaiva funeral)

Societies with an accentuated fractal and dividual understanding of the world acknowledge that aspects of the person come from specific places in the cosmos and return there after death. As well as illustrating the temporal nature of personhood, this also denotes that the aspects of the person can be mapped spatially within the cosmos. Certain places might be associated with spirits, ghosts, or the bodies of the dead. An ethnographic study will serve as an example of the fate of the dividual/partible person, and their relocation and reconfiguration after death.

Iteanu (1988, 1995) and Barraud *et al.* (1994) describe four facets of personhood recognized among the Papuan Orokaiva. These emerge at different stages in existence. First, the *ahihi*, or 'image', which exists as soon as a child is born, but is submerged during life, to be released again (and stay present) from the moment of death until mourning ceases. The *ahihi* is associated with and may become attached to material things, particularly feathers and shell goods, and is illustrated by wealth objects at funerals. Second, the *hamo*, which is the contingent historical identity of the social person in life. The *hamo* is built up of 'the various social relations created . . . through the rituals and of the "physical" marks like scars, body size, special decorations, names, emblems, familial affiliations and so forth, associated to these relations' (Iteanu 1995: 139). The *hamo* is accumulative, and broadly equates to a biography of social relations and experiences. Once the *hamo* is removed, the person's name, and stories about them, cease to be verbalized. Instead, their histories are now recalled through the objects, places, and events which are the entwined features of their biographies. The *hamo* may be also manifested and memorialized in the body of pigs at ceremonial events (Barraud *et al.* 1994: 34). Their social person is therefore embedded in memory and material culture. Third, the *jo* is the 'inside' of a person. This quality is unknowable by others, and does not correspond with our conception of individuality. Indeed, *jo* often emerges during *jape* rituals when people behave as supernatural entities, and witchcraft involves the extension of *jo* out of a person (Iteanu 1988). Such witchcraft is not always a conscious undertaking in Melanesia. *Jo* is something of a shapeless chaotic force that is brought to light briefly in rituals, then hidden again, and manifestations of *jo* are to be found in discrete gifts people sometimes give each other. The *jo* does not survive the death process. Finally, there is the *onderi*, which is not emergent during life. This is an anonymous, collective state the person attains after death, after the period of mourning for their *hamo* ends. The state of *onderi* is only fully attained once the biography of the individual facet of the person has been forgotten. The *onderi* take on the forms of wild animals, and are anonymous, nameless, because they have no kin relations with the living (Iteanu 1995: 146). Iteanu is also quite specific that these should not be seen as 'ancestors', since their kin relations with the living have been effectively severed.

Since people are continually dying, there are always different sorts of spirits present in the Orokaiva world. For example, the *ahihi* can be considered as the spirit of the dead, and is produced through removing and transforming the *hamo*. The *ahihi* is a partible component of the person, therefore, and is still identified with the deceased it was separated from. During the mortuary cycle mourners may take the possessions of the deceased and swear an oath on this memento to undertake a taboo. The *ahihi* is tethered to such objects, and can be summoned to do the bidding of the new owner as long as the taboo is maintained (Iteanu 1995: 145). *Ahihi* are summoned through using objects, usually to protect other objects; their whole existence is centred around material culture: things with spirits and efficacy, things that retain a part of the dead person they were separated from by death. If we were to map all of the qualities of the Orokaiva person in a static way we might say that wild spirits live in the forest and are non-human, while objects are visited by spirits that were recently human. But at other points in time these spirits were within people, making up a part of the whole person and the community. The fractal person is relocated after death from the level of the individual to the cosmos. Facets of the person can exist both in human bodies and in the wider world. Personal life could be presented as a process, so that the person is finally completed after death, but then undone again as the process of transformation throughout existence continues. Personal qualities exist in all material things, and after death some of these features endure in things and animals: the dead are transformed to ancestral essence (image), to temporary spirits of things, and into wild animals. Things and animals previously encapsulated by the deceased are redistributed and become encapsulated by other living persons. Furthermore, particular places (e.g. the wild forest) can become associated with particular features of the person.

This ethnography suggests that the person is relocated spatially and temporally after death, not as a whole but as an aggregate of different features. The redistribution of the person traditionally involved the remains of the dead themselves. While we might imagine that the person would go on to an afterlife intact, therefore, this is not the fate of a dividual and partible person. However, even in these instances, the requirement to separate the dead from the living is evident, and the individuality of the deceased is mourned. Funerals often remember the dead by presenting a temporarily complete version of the person:

> Just as the person in life dispenses wealth to kinsfolk and partners and thus achieves social identity, so when the person dies a last recognition, or else a re-creation of those 'parts' which he or she demonstrated while active, must be put in hand.
>
> (Strathern 1981: 219)

However, it is not only in the gathering together of the whole that the deceased is remembered:

[Wiru] men and women wore bones of kin or spouses round their necks; the bones of a baby which died might be hung up in a netbag and kept for some months, wrapped in sweet-smelling grasses while its mother mourned her loss. Skulls were kept and placed collectively in a hamlet or village-based cult house . . .

(Strathern 1981: 212)

Mortuary gatherings in Melanesia involve a host of exchanges, which further redistribute and relocate the deceased, and redirect relations among survivors. Mourning extends to all of those who had lost a part of their person with the deceased. So, following the presentation of the gathered corpse, including the human body, the dividual and partible character of the person is then presenced in mortuary exchanges where these redistributions occur (e.g. the 'Are'are: see Box 2.1; or the Sabarl corpses of axes and food that are redistributed through mortuary ceremonies: see Battaglia 1990: 177–81). Mortuary rites often involve far-reaching sets of exchanges among the community, carried out over a series of years. These both return the aspects of the person to the communities that contributed to them – for example, by relocating bodies given in marriage by another kin group – and form a new bond between those communities. The mortuary process is therefore one in which relationships are separated and re-articulated just as in any other exchange. Mourners identify with the deceased – they have lost a part of themselves – and may take the 'qualities of death' into their person through funerary dress and performance (Munn 1986: 167). However, many successive mortuary feasts are performed in Melanesia, extending many years after initial death. The process of separation and reconfiguration is ongoing, renewing social relations and, along with other cycles of exchange, ensures the flow of substance through the world.

Mortuary exchanges alter the nature and status of the deceased, and may even eventually enhance their influence in the land of the living. Strathern (1981) argues that Melpa mortuary exchanges do not serve to negate inheritance, nor to completely forget and undo the dead; instead these practices affirm the social relations in which the deceased was involved. Those who do not give at Melpa funerals will not participate in further exchanges in the full mortuary cycle where they might receive gifts from the kin of the deceased; they are effectively opting out of the social network of the deceased. Yet the majority of survivors continue that network of relations through repeated ceremonial mortuary exchanges held sporadically over many years. Furthermore, *moka* cycles of gift exchange that may develop out of these mortuary cycles form an enduring replication and embellishment to the remembered identity of the deceased. Repeated patterns of giving and speaking become associated with the dead:

> In Hagen . . . the person can be replicated and magnified after death through the extension of exchanges which can follow death itself; a war-hero's death may be paid for over and over again, to echo in the speeches of men for generations.
>
> (Strathern 1981: 219)

If a person is killed by a member of another group, it is not the deceased, but the death that is remembered in ongoing exchanges between the clans (Strathern 1981: 210). Mortuary exchanges can therefore continue old social relations, seemingly put at risk by the death of an individual, and are vital spheres for interaction between clan groups. Relations between genders are also re-articulated through dealing with the dead in Melanesia, some of whose substance is owed to each parental line and each gender. Gimi women transform the corpses of men by removing female flesh from the male bones of the dead, 'consuming' it back into the female lineage and freeing a spiritual aspect of the person to roam the forest, which is a male domain (Strathern 1982). The plurally gendered dividual person is therefore made partible, separated out and returned to several points of origin. The result is the recycling of personal essences within the community and the cosmos. Such events need not be without a political side: the 'ownership' of the corpse or body parts might be contested by different lineages for example: in a patrilocal society should a woman's corpse pass to her mother's, brother's, or husband's clan (see Vitebsky 1993: 49; Bloch 1971)?

The physical bodies of the dead were traditionally fragmented in Melanesia. However, Melanesian partible persons may be buried in single graves – although in some cases this is temporary and remains may be later exhumed (e.g. Hirsch 1990; Maschio 1994: 88–93, 186–9). The exact format of funerals varies. Reay (1959) records the fragmentation of shell goods on the body of the Kuma deceased. Although Strathern (1981: 220) has not observed this among Hagen communities he argues that wealth must not be taken away by the dead intact, nor passed on directly to any single heir, but rather redistributed throughout the community. The materiality of death is therefore closely bound up with the practices and principles structuring personhood, even if the corpse is kept intact. Since colonial contact many Melanesians have buried their dead. Changes in beliefs and social practices may therefore not immediately oust and replace prior practices and beliefs, though they may supplement them and gradually reconfigure them. Overall, then, it is not essential that the body of a dividual/partible person be fragmented, although such practices are frequently a key feature of such modes of personhood.

Death as sacrifice and cosmogony: transformation of the Hindu person

The Hindu permeable person is almost always cremated, and burial is not practised. Cremation takes place on sacrificial grounds, next to running water. The immolation of the dead is in fact an act of sacrifice (Parry 1994; Ghosh 1989: 137), and the dead are not really dead at all until the cremation is underway and the skull cracked. The fire transforms and refines the substance-codes of the body so that they 'then assume their subtle forms', while the soul is carried to Heaven by the smoke (Ghosh 1989: 141). The remains are further refined or purified by immersion in water, frequently through scattering remains in a sacred river.

The Hindu person is fractal, and the death of the person is equivalent to the end of the universe, which also takes the form of a fire followed by a flood (Parry 1994: 30–1). 'Cremation is cosmogony; and an individual death is assimilated into the process of cosmic regeneration' (Parry 1994: 31). This destruction is also a rebirth, then, since Hindu conceptions of time tie the end of one universe to the beginning of another. Death and the recreation of the universe are united, so that death is a process of cosmogony or universe creation and renewal brought about by a metaphorical human sacrifice. The body contains and is equivalent to the universe, and to the Holy City which is the most direct gateway to Heaven, the most effective locale for these transformations, since it was here that Vishnu sat aflame and created the universe (ibid.). Hindu sacrificial death ensures the recycling of substance-codes of all kinds, distilled out of the fractal person. The bodies of kings and living saints are more potent, encompassing more of the cosmos, and given special rites (Oestigaard in press).

Hindu funerals remove the corpse from society, and seek to separate and sever the deceased from social relations. The intention is to dissolve any sense of individuality fully, and to reconfigure social relations. The person is bounded yet permeable, and boundaries must be completely overflowed in death. While in the west the bounded individual is 'gone' once death intervenes, here the person must be killed through social action, and their boundaries visibly permeated for a final time. Components of the dividual self are separated, releasing the soul to heaven and reincarnation, but also a ghost which must be transformed into an anonymous ancestor through successive rites (Parry 1994: ch. 6). The dead person is not commemorated with any memorial, and offerings given some days after cremation are dedicated not only to the specific deceased but also to their parents and grandparents (Ghosh 1989: 147). A part of the recent dead also becomes a ghost or spirit, and in parts of India relations with these entities must be carefully negotiated. Spirits may possess the living, or the bodies of objects and animals. The Indian Sora conduct seances in which the dead inhabit the bodies of the living, speaking through them (Vitebsky 1993). The dead may permeate the dividual vessels that are the bodies of the living. Only when they are reassured about their relations with the living will they leave for the spirit world. The Sora discourse on and with the dead illustrates that the dead are not easily separated from society, or the world of the living. Even when a major element of the dead person is destined to go elsewhere other aspects of the dead linger in society, and spirits of the newly dead are present. The permeable person is made partible through death, so that all of the remaining substance-codes they drew together in life are absolutely refined and relocated in the recreation of the universe. The social mode of personhood prevalent here, permeability, is also stressed in mortuary practices: the fires permeate the body and free the soul, which glides away. The refined remains are washed downstream with the flow of the river to permeate the cosmos. Again, while absence of these features does not negate the possibility of permeability as a key feature of personhood, their presence may suggest a conception of the person as permeable or partible. While the meanings of social technologies that dismember or cremate the corpse, or allow it to decay, are never transparent, then, their interpretation in the context of the wider circulation of materials and treatment of bodies and objects may suggest the presence of structuring principles like partibility and permeability.

Box 4.1 Funerary practices, social order, sacrifice and communication with the divine in Iron Age southern Scandinavia

Mortuary practices may involve human bodies in exchange networks between the living human world and the spiritual world. Human communities are often indebted to supernatural entities for their continuing existence. Returning the dead to the cosmos is one way of repaying that debt. Recently, Terje Oestigaard (1999, 2000) has suggested that the bodies of the dead in Iron Age southern Scandianavia

continued on facing page

were prepared like food to be consumed by divine beings. He describes how corpses could be 'butchered' and disarticulated, thereby served raw. They could also be 'cooked' through boiling in cauldrons or through cremation, and 'burnt' through cremation and the burning of naked bones. Different proportions of collagen remain in bones depending on the temperatures to which they have been exposed (Holck 1987). Holck's analysis has indicated that some bones which appeared unburnt were actually 'cooked' or 'burnt' to different degrees (1987: 136–9), and one set of bones showing no signs of heating exhibited cut-marks. Oestigaard (2000) argues that these ways of preparing the bodies of the dead relate to religious practice, particularly sacrifice. For example, placing cremated remains in urns might transform them into a gift, just as a pot might contain food to be given away (Oestigaard 2000: 50; cf. Lucas 1996: 113). Different deities may have been invoked in different mortuary techniques and different kinds of death, such as stabbing, hanging and drowning (Oestigaard 2000: 51). Multiple acts of violence causing death were often carried out on Iron Age bog bodies, which were sometimes strangled, poisoned or had their throats cut, and/or were clubbed to death (M. Williams 2003: 94); again, perhaps offering different elements of the person and community to distinct deities. As we will see in the next chapter, features of the person, like souls, are not necessarily singular and indivisible. Some practices might be reserved for particular categories of person so that high-ranking or famous warriors might be recovered from the battlefield, cremated and returned home in urns while others would be left for scavengers or buried near the battlefield (Oestigaard 2000: 52). In each case the transformation of the person after death may relate to their standing and social relations in life, on the one hand, but also depended on the interests of other community members, which seemingly extended to the deliberate killing of at least those

continued on next page

bodies recovered from bogs. The location of the dead was also significant in that different deities might exist in the sky or the underworld, contacted through cremation and deposition respectively. Each means of transformation may convey essences between the community and supernatural powers, repay debts, regenerate a feature of the world. Since people can be gifts, like objects, the destruction or sacrifice of a person can be seen as a dedicatory act, transferring human substance to the supernatural powers and fulfilling exchange relations with those powers. Just as humans consumed food which may have had divine origins, so the gods consumed elements of human beings.

Summary: modes of personhood, ways of death

In summary, the three modes of personhood considered here each have distinctive ways of death. Western individuality is supported by the conservation of a memory of the intact person, especially the body in which western personhood resides. Possessions intimate to them may be passed on, but the substances and essences of the person are not transferable. Melanesian personhood, drawing on partibility, induces the complete fragmentation of the person after death, historically including the body. People become a number of entities after death, and disperse into the social and material world. The physical parts of the person are socially circulated, often for some time, and carry aspects of the deceased with them. Hindu permeable personhood draws the elements that create and compose the universe, like fire and water, through the person, refining the substance-codes they encapsulate. The parts of the body are not kept as specific objects in distinct places, but permeate the universe generally, sent into the sky or down the river. The bounded person is unbounded. Both of these dividual ways of death suit the predominant relations of personhood, but do not deny the concurrent presence of more individual features. Mortuary rites often draw together a person's world of relations and present them as a whole, temporarily finished entity:

as we would see it, present a vision of the individual. Many features of the person may be separated and relocated after death, though some features may remain, including ghosts. Ancestral beings of different sorts may be produced through successive rituals: in some cases these commemorate individual achievements, in others they do not; in some cases the ancestor is commemorated physically, in others only by memory or ephemeral actions.

Contesting death

Why death is not an inversion of life, but part of the social negotiation of life

So far we have established that mortuary rites deconstitute the person, and that they also provide opportunities for the reconstitution of social relations among the survivors. In some cases, they also compose the dead as a different kind of entity, or renew the cosmos as a whole. However, the dead may simply stay dead, and may be inversions of normal life. How are we to negotiate this complex situation?

Judith Okely's (1979) ethnography of late twentieth-century British gypsies illustrated that mobility was core to the identity of living gypsies. Death relocated the deceased to such an extent that they were no longer a part of gypsy society at all, and did not go to an afterlife (Okely 1979: 87). This was demonstrated by the removal of the deceased from the gypsy community entirely. Instead, the dead – and the dying – cross over into the world of the *gorgios*, or non-gypsies. Gypsy dead are therefore buried in *gorgio* cemeteries. Just as the polluted body of the dead is taken out of society, so is the property of the deceased: caravans may be burnt or sold (Okely 1979: 88). The *mulo*, spirit of the dead, is seen as attached to these possessions, and to the corpse. This spirit is malignant, and must be excised from society. It is also mobile in a way, like living gypsies, and its ostracism is effected through these acts of destruction, and by grounding it in place. Archaeologists often warn that death inverts life, and that direct interpretations of the treatment of the dead may not reflect the world of the living; these are after all ideological statements (Shennan 1982; Shanks and Tilley 1982). The gypsy way of death does invert life; however, there is an absolutely holistic relation between life and death. In everyday life it is the *gorgios* who are beyond society, who are the inverse of gypsy life, and so the dead join their communities. The distinction between the living and the dead is identified in relation to the gypsy and the *gorgio* world. While treatment in death in this case inverts practices among the living, it also identifies a set of principles and practices continually undertaken by the living in dealing with both the *gorgio* world *and* dealing with the dead: separation and avoidance. Okely's study therefore reveals a relationship between personhood, ethnicity and death. The gypsies focused on the relation between themselves and the *gorgios* in transforming the living into the dead, explicitly ethnicizing the deceased.

Therefore, death replaces one state of personhood with another, which may be at odds with the personhood of the living. The dead may be reincorporated into society, or pushed into another community, either of foreigners or the dead, or spiritual entities, wild animals and places, or a mixture of these. All of these activities are social and political as well as spiritual or religious, and they can reveal a great deal about the generation and dissipation of personhood. While they do not directly cite the individual identity of the deceased, nor present the corpse in a way that allows reconstruction of the total notion of personhood prevalent in a community, they do employ the same principles and practices that are deployed in generating personhood elsewhere. Clearly there is no stock way to detect exactly *how* personhood or personal identity are cited in mortuary practice. Shanks and Tilley (1982) provide an archaeological example of the argument that the treatment of the dead is an ideological statement that inverts lived experience. They argue that the communalisation of human bones in earlier Neolithic chambered tombs and mortuary structures was part of an ideological assertion that all were equal after death. In fact, they insist, this masked real social inequalities. During this period the remains of the dead in central southern England were frequently circulated among the community

(Thomas 1999a). Control over remains in socially and spiritually liminal locales like chambered cairns, mortuary structures or causewayed enclosures might have been a contested issue, but remains are also found outside of those contexts, and intermixed with broken objects and parts of animals' bodies in pits (Thomas 1999a: 68).

Human remains were a key part of the organization of depositional practices, in a variety of contexts. It would seem unlikely that death and the dead formed an isolated sphere of interaction which was ideologically at odds with other everyday social relations. In fact, citations of personhood made through the remains of the dead do not so much mask conflicts and differences as form a media for their negotiation – the result is neither a reflection of reality nor a polished mask to cover it. Access to the bones of the dead may have been not only a spiritual act but a highly political arena. Bone may have illustrated the presence of the dead in the world of the living, and combinations of substances including human bone a vital part of the renewal of relations within the cosmos. For this reason, while it is crucial to be wary of making direct interpretations from the treatment of the dead, it is also misleading to treat interaction with the dead as an anomalous practice or a one-off event. All material remains form media used again and again in social and political interaction, and are subject to differing fields of social practice (Barrett 2001). In European prehistory the remains of the dead were frequently re-accessed and reused repeatedly, sometimes many centuries after their initial deposition. Personhood was continually renegotiated through material media, including the reuse of past remains. Even the reassembly of old bones became significant at some chambered cairns for a host of reasons involving social politics over the nature of personhood (e.g. Fowler 2001; Thomas 1999a: 151) and, we might even suggest, spiritual regeneration through reconfiguring parts to make new potent wholes (see Chapter 5). Logics of personhood were reflected upon, exercised and revised precisely through these media, and the dead played a fully interactive role in the ongoing negotiation of Neolithic personhood.

Conclusion

Death is a transformation of the person, and conceptions of this transformation are integral to understandings of personhood. Mortuary practices effect a modulation in personhood from, for example, dividuality to partibility, or indivisibility to extreme separation. These are, however, part of the overall mode of personhood; they are prefigured transformations. It is easy to be drawn into considering the fate of the individual after death, but predominant structures of personhood often overwhelm consideration of individuality here. The dissolution and redistribution of the person is frequently a community concern with important cosmological consequences. In this chapter we have seen how personal relations among the living are reworked alongside the transformation of the dead person, including through manipulating the remains of the dead. These include human remains, but also other vestiges of past lives. However, these redistributions can only be understood with reference to the wider social context. The decomposition and recomposition of the person are constant features of social life in partible relations, and the treatment of the dead merely exposes this logic through the literal decomposition of the body. The broader ongoing circulation of the essences that sustain personhood throughout society and the cosmos forms the subject of the next chapter.

5

BODIES, SUBSTANCES
AND COMMUNITY

Introduction

We have already investigated how objects may contain the same qualities and have the same effects as people, and how they may emerge out of persons and as persons in their own right. We have also seen how the components of the dead are relocated throughout the universe. Vitally charged substances and qualities may also interpenetrate people throughout life, and we have already seen how important maintaining such flows is in the maintenance and transformation of personhood. This chapter focuses on the transmission of substances between bodies and through the cosmos as a way towards understanding the connection between the human and non-human in societies that accentuate relational concepts of the person. As we will see, this is one of the greatest differences between indivisible individuals and dividual personhood. Partibility will be revealed as a feature of societies other than Melanesian ones, though made sensible through rather different conceptions of the person and cosmos, and the general permeability of people will be suggested as an equally widespread phenomenon. Overall, it will be argued that relational and dividual personhood involves the continual production, consumption and circulation of essences out of which persons are produced.

Bodies and the transmission of substance

The control and circulation of substances is a fundamental matter in the generation and modification of personhood. This section illustrates how bodies are conceptualized as separate entities, or as connected to one another, depending on how substance is produced and transmitted, and what qualities are attributed to the materials of the body and the world. The conception and production of specific kinds of body is a matter of recent interest to archaeologists (e.g. Yates 1993; Chapman 1996, 2000; Hamilakis *et al.* 2002; Joyce 2000; Meskell 1996, 1999; Fowler 2001; Thomas 2002). Here it will be argued that patterns in how the boundaries of bodies are mediated, and how connections between them are effected, reveal a great deal about personhood in any cultural context. More precise definitions of substances and essences will be offered later.

Substance, form and the public body

'Personification' . . . might be better understood as consumption that converts food and objects and people into *other* people.

(Battaglia 1990: 191, discussing Sabarl personhood)

The monitoring of the shape and content of the body is a frequent cultural concern. Consumption and the absorption of substances are often publicly monitored through the appearance of the body. Strathern (1999: 45, 48–51) describes how the Etoro kill babies who are 'too fat' since their bodies are evidence of sorcery and the hoarding of life energies. Fijians monitor each other's bodies closely for signs of weight loss, an indicator of collective social failure, since each body manifests the well-being of society (Becker 1995). Eating together, from the same bowl, is a medium for the transfer of saliva between husband and wife among the Marianad (Busby 1997, 1999). Montague (1989) describes how the Kaduwagan 'eat for each other', including their dead, rather than directly nourishing their own bodies. In short, the monitoring of consumption is the public regulation of the body, and the flows that pass through the person have social, physical and magical effects (see Boyd 2002; Hamilakis 2002; Meskell 1999: 46–50). Identities are also shaped and transformed through dress, the appearance of the body, and the performance of bodily movements (e.g. Joyce 2000). Bodily decoration is constitutive of specific identities for ceremonial events in New Guinea, and it is common for personal decoration to change the nature of the person 'all the way down'. Not all societies see the body as the primary facet of the person, and the spirit might be described as immutable while the body is subject to reconfiguration according to the relationship in which it is engaged (e.g. Csordas 1999: 143–4). To change personal appearance may, at many times in the past, have been to change personal identity, to obtain a different perspective and a different sense of self. Technologies that dress the body and monitor bodily boundaries are vital to understanding these relational effects. The bodies of the living are often marked or covered to protect boundaries and orifices, and to regulate the movement of essences – something only necessary if the person is permeable to some degree. This can vary from wearing clothing to cover orifices (e.g. Tuareg veils as membranes to monitor possession by spirits, the boundaries between men and women, and expressions of emotion – Rasmussen 1995), to Polynesian tattoos which limit the effect of the body's innate sacredness and potency (Gell 1993). Many Maori chiefs, high-ranking women and priests are not tattooed since they are highly potent, and retain openness to flows of energy – but they are therefore also dangerous nodes in the cosmos (Gell 1993: 259–66). Other chiefs are tattooed precisely to contain this sanctity (ibid.: 211). Tattooing stops potency from leaching out and affecting others, desanctifying the body. The manipulation of substances and monitoring of bodily boundaries is a cultural and public matter, central to concepts of the person. The regulation of boundaries is a key indicator in understanding whether the person is best thought of as indivisible, or whether permeability and partibility are matters of public concern. For archaeologists, it may often be misleading to understand body-forming processes as expressions

of individuality at the cost of overlooking the communal negotiation of these other fields of personhood. While body-forming
practices do individuate, then, they may not be expressions of
individuality from the inside out.

Substance and the emergence of the indivisible body

During the medieval period in Europe the person was thought of
as a complex and, we could argue, fairly dividual and permeable
entity. Aside from the mind and soul, the body was a vessel that
also contained several humours. These humours flowed around
the body, and were manifest in the phlegm (watery), black bile
(earthy), yellow bile (fiery), and blood (airy) (Rawcliffe 1995:
33). Each humour affected the character of the person in a different
way; sanguine people had an excess of blood, and were therefore
cheerful rather than melancholy or bad-tempered, for instance.
Substances were poured into and out of the body. People were
bled or given vomit-inducing concoctions to alter the balance of
substances in their body and to affect their mood and personality;
but changes in external conditions, including astrological ones,
could also influence the body (Rawcliffe 1995: 59–70). Affected
by changes in such substances and conditions, the body was
permeable to outside influences, including evil ones. Medieval
witchcraft-avoidance tactics involved the burying or walling up
of garments intimate to the body (like shoes or undergarments,
often belonging to vulnerable children), or *exuviae* (things which
are both part of the body and also detachable from it like hair,
skin cells, nails, sweat, mucous, urine and faeces, and sexual
fluids). Those concerned about witchcraft were careful to burn
hair or nails that had been cut. Witchcraft could wither the
unseen aspects of the person, like fertility or the soul itself,
through contact with bodily substances or by otherwise magically
permeating the person.

By the time of the Scientific Revolution this elemental notion of
the body was joined by a mechanical conception of the body and
the properties within. Just as Descartes had distinguished the stuff
of the body from the matter of the world, so Thomas Hobbes

(1588–1679) saw the body as a discrete machine fully determined by its structure (what we would see as its physical composition, anatomy or physiology, and chemistry). The mind was simply an extension of that structure, an emergent property of the motions of bodily organs, and the soul did not exist (Morris 1991: 17). Hobbes's material determinism reduced the character of the person to something that is biologically innate, governed by the matter and form of the body. This perspective was a precursor to the idea that personality is dictated by a set of needs which are transmitted in our genetic material, and the idea that the body with its brain is 'hardwired' with a set of desires which all individuals share. Hobbes was formulating an emergent materialist metaphor for understanding bodies as machines (Morris 1991: 21). The whole world could be thought about in this materialist and mechanical way, reduced to the properties of its substances. Later medical and biological interest in the body led to anatomical studies performed through human dissections. The size and shape – and gender – of specific organs were held materially responsible for particular character traits (Jordanova 1989). The indivisible person was increasingly locked into the body, even though personality could still be influenced by external adjustment to internal chemistry or mechanics.

The machine as a social technology became paramount during the Industrial Revolution, along with widespread use of the mechanic conception of the body. However, organic understandings of the body were repeatedly revised and have risen to dominance in the last 200 years. Darwin's evolutionary theory provided a revolutionary understanding of organisms (Darwin 1859), and led to the development of ideas about genetics. Darwin's theory of evolution pertained only to biological organisms, but has since been applied to thinking about society (Spencer 1857), material culture (e.g. in Pitt Rivers's typological method; Gosden 1999: 28), and even ideas and culture (Dawkins 1976; Dennett 1995; Sperber 1996). These latter theories are concerned with the transmission of ideas in a similar way to genes, and the transmission of form from generation to generation. We could think of these as cultural theories about the transmission of particular substance-codes: from genes to 'memes' (units of thought). 'Meme' theory perhaps recognizes thoughts and practices as something akin to Marriott's substance-codes that may be transmitted between individuals, though those individuals have little say in the matter. However, genetic theories only trace the flow of substances from body to body by descent.

Transmission of substance as descent

Since western individuals are relatively indivisible we rarely give away a physical part of ourselves. Other than through blood transfusions, organ donation, and similar practices, our bodily substances are generally transmitted only through procreation. The connection between blood donor and recipient is not personal and direct. The indivisible person transmits generative substance during reproduction, not in normal relations with others. Children are related to parents by 'blood', and blood-lines are measured through family trees: this reckoning of descent can be called cladistic or dendritic. Cladistics map lineage and direct descent in a unilinear fashion that Ingold (2000c: 136) calls a genealogical model of relatedness. Personal substance (e.g. DNA) is transmitted from one generation to the next (Ingold 2000c: 137). The linearity of relations means there can be no real engagement with the dead, and no revisiting past relations. All substance is tangible, and therefore it makes no sense to refer to knowledge as a substance.

Transmission of substances in ongoing relations

Ingold (2000c) argues that many non-western communities transmit substances between bodies rather differently. These same communities are likely to include spiritual beings, often in the form of animals, the dead, and plants or even rocks, within the pool of persons that they habitually engage with. Generative qualities and substances are not transmitted from one generation to another biologically but are exchanged between the different entities incorporated into the community at any point in time

106

(Ingold 2000c: 144–6). Ingold, following Deleuze and Guattari, refers to such relations as rhizomes, conceptualizing them as the roots of an imaginary plant: each root may grow back into others, rejoining branches separated earlier in the growth process. The dead are not fully removed from society, and interaction with all beings is dialogic. Substance, energy and knowledge can be gained from sources other than the living human community, and transmitted in other ways than through biological reproduction. For example, Peter Thomas (1999), studying kinship and conception among the Tenamambondro of south-east Madagascar, has argued that the transmission of gendered essences from generation to generation was a secondary concern to the transmission of practical knowledge about the continual manipulation of these substances. It is more important to the Tenamambondro to pass on knowledge and, above all, practices and techniques from one generation to another than it is to pass on one's 'blood' in a direct line of biological descent. Adopted children are common. Flows of qualities between people did take place, but these were more likely to happen through contact with objects within a lifetime (e.g. through sharing a meal) than through the blood-lines of a descent lineage (i.e. through reproduction). Knowing how to carry out these interactions gave each person the ability to relate to any other. Here, linear, cladistic biological descent is not the most important relationship through which features of identity are transmitted. People in relational paradigms should not simply be understood as 'procreated entities, connected to one another along lines of genealogical connection or *relatedness*, but rather as centres of progenerative activity variously positioned within an all-encompassing field of *relationships*' (Ingold 2000c: 144, original emphasis). Among the Lio of Indonesia, the exchange of enduring gold valuables that are inalienable from a 'house' community ensures continuity through alliances over the long term (Howell 1989). The 'house' is a social unit that is not reducible to a descent group, and 'house' members include things as well as human beings. It is the future generations of the 'house' who will reap the benefits of such a gift given in the lifetime of any one community member, who may not themselves live to see the return gift. Gold is imbued with the essences of the 'house' and is inalienable from the process of life renewal as a whole. In these cases, and others, descent lineages *may* still play a role, but how they are structured and negotiated may be fluid, and both objects and the dead are major forces in the renewal of vital energies among the community. In short, patterns in practical deployment of material things and substances may be the most important feature of social transmission.

We return to some implications of these forms of generation and distinctions between two different kinds of non-western generative logics later in the chapter, but this mode of thought is appropriate to fractal and dividual notions of personhood. These relations give rise to people rather different to the atomistic individual, for, although all relations are negotiable, those doing the negotiating are not just human beings and the very materials of their person may be at stake.

Metaphor and fractals: human bodies alongside others

Substances with generative qualities are not just circulated between human bodies but can be circulated among the world at large, and can be found contained in the bodies of buildings, objects, plants and animals. We can therefore see that dividual relations not only conjoin human beings but all of the elements of the world within a person. These may all be connected by the same pattern of transformations, and a metaphorical scheme is often apparent linking the treatment of human bodies, substances, objects, places, animals and plants. The same logic applies to transactions at all scales, across all entities, and this logic relies on metaphorical constructions (for a full exploration of the role of metaphor in understanding the material world see Tilley 1999). Strathern (1988, 1992a) suggests that anthropological interpretations are most effective if they draw on the indigenous metaphors that equally explain people and the world. This seems an admirable goal for archaeologists (see Brück 2001a; Tilley 1996: ch. 6, and 1999). Metaphors are inseparable from the social technologies and material practices that are fundamental to any particular society. These include food production. The concealed growth of pigs and root crops, their display at key exchanges and their eventual redistribution form key media in the development of people in parts of Melanesia (e.g. Strathern 1998: 145; Munn 1986). Elsewhere, the human life-cycle may be measured against the growth of plants and trees, such as palms on Bali (Giambelli 1998: 140–1). The substances of the palm tree are comparable to different bodily substances, and coconuts are deposited filled with human substances during rites of passage (e.g. placenta following childbirth, ashes following cremation). Maschio (1994: 181) outlines how coconut palms are grown from the ribcages of the Rauto dead. Tree crops may mark out relations of kinship and belonging (e.g. in the giving of coconuts), and are processed in keeping with the life-cycle of people they are associated with. The substances of humans and plants are sometimes entwined, and feed into one another. Ingold (2000a) describes several instances of metaphors of growth extended equally both to people – particularly children – and plants and animals. Seasonal cycles in activity, rates of growth and processes of ageing can all be measured in step with or in contrast to these natural cycles. Ideas of regeneration and rebirth or of cyclical existence also tie in human substances, social regeneration and the fertility of the land. Among the Merina in Madagascar, the body is buried so that the wet 'female' flesh can return to the earth near the village, and the body is dried out in its temporary grave (see Box 5.1). The dessicated remains are taken to ancestral tombs, where the dried male bones eventually become 'earth' (Bloch 1982: 215). The generative substances of the land and the body are tied together in a continuous cycle. Such comparability of substances and generative processes may extend to a host of social technologies, including metalworking (Tilley 1999: 57–9). Trends in social activity permeate entirely any subject–object divide we may construct: in fact, in many cases these parallel life-cycles of people and things are not metaphors at all. Plants and other materials may be conceptualized as integrated in a holistic system that makes the inside of the body intelligible through its interrelations with the outside. In fact, such notions of inside and outside may themselves be articulated in successively different ways through exchange and consumption (e.g. Strathern 1998). One person may have elements 'within' another (see Chapters 2 and 3). A fractal person can therefore potentially encompass all of the components of society and the cosmos.

Box 5.1 The Malagasy house

The Madagascan Malagasy house is equivalent to the person, and its body is subject to similar material transformations as human persons and their relationships (Bloch 1995). The house is built following marriage, a point when young, highly mobile people settle down, literally and meta-phorically. Initially the structure is flimsy, and, apart from the central posts, made from green wood. This structure is gradually consolidated over the years, replaced with more durable wood. The hardening of the Malagasy house empha-sizes the gradual fixing of an identity which originates in the coming together of two or more sources (Bloch 1995: 214–15). This can be compared with the drying out of the body in Madagascar. The body of a child is flimsy, fresh, and seen as wet: the fluids that composed it have yet to con-geal. The body dries out and hardens through life. Following death, stones may be raised in memory of the ancestral dead; they stand not only for the dead individual but for the firm-ness of the relations that produced that person. Even though the person is dead, their presence remains, pinning together different segments of society. The fully hardened substances of the house also demonstrate the enduring nature of a body which is also a relationship (Bloch 1995: 214–15). The longer such relations between lines exist, the firmer they become. The same structuring principles are enacted through discourses on the human body, on marriage, and on the cycle of life and death through material structures, including houses and also monuments (see Parker Pearson

continued on facing page

---

and Ramilisonina 1998). Building and living with a Malagasy house reifies a particular understanding of what it means to be a person and to be part of a family; indeed, these cannot be fully separated out from each other as concepts. The Malagasy house is a material condensation of a relationship, not a passive metaphor for the body. Equivalent substances constitute people and houses, so that the hardwood house posts are called bones, and the house has been grown. Decorations that adorn the house are not symbols with abstract meaning, but marks that beautify the house much as a body might be decorated. So to a certain extent it does not matter whether we attribute the epithet of 'person' fully to the house; it conveys the relations core to the entirety of Malagasy social life, and tells us a great deal about Malagasy personhood at a scale greater than the singular person.

Unmediated exchange, dividuality, and the transmission of substance

Next we turn to the mechanics of what may count as a substance, how substances are transmitted in relational forms of personhood, and what effects such processes may have. Strathern creates a distinction between mediated and unmediated exchange for Highland New Guinea societies (Strathern 1988: 178–207). Unmediated exchanges are those that take place as transferrals between dividual people that involve no external material culture. Body parts are not transformed into objects that are extracted; rather, bodily substance, words, or unseen spiritual essences are transmitted directly. Unmediated exchanges do not rely on an objectified and singularized object. Instead, these are 'gift exchange[s] without a gift' (Strathern 1988: 179), and have immediate effects on the recipient who feels the impact in their person directly. Unmediated relations, like feeding, growing, talking and sexual intercourse, can be used to reproduce already existing relations and make them physically manifest: a child becomes a substitute or direct replica of the relations between the parents' families. Unmediated exchange, then, is the means for the direct transmission of substance within families and clans (e.g. the transmission of essences in initiation rites; Strathern 1988: 208–24). Chains of transmission link one generation to the next, though not just during original biological conception, and coalesce in the dividual person. People and things are thereby presented as dividual conduits for substantial relations. It should also be stressed that mediated and unmediated exchanges are connected. In fact, Strathern (1988: 264) presents sacrifice of gifts as a form of mediation with ancestral ghosts and other powers. She argues that sacrifice bridges mediated and unmediated exchange: the gift is given as an object, but is destroyed – it cannot be grown and returned. Instead, the desired return gift takes an unmediated form: the power of the spiritual beings that will sustain the living. Sacrifice is therefore a transformation that bridges two spheres of social activity, and is a collective, communal undertaking. In all forms of Melanesian exchange, then, essences or qualities like fertility may move equally through the human body, through substances, through the mediation of objects, or by exchanges with non-human powers.

It is necessary at this point to reinstate the distinction between qualities and substances that Marriott's (1976) concept of substance-codes conjoins. In Indian thought, substances are coded as hot or cold, male or female. Yet in Melanesia substances have relational or ambiguous forces within them: generative power that might be male or female or both. Melanesian substances may be coded differently in successive contexts: they are ambiguous but then activated as male or female, for instance. The transmission of substances discussed so far could be reframed as the transmission of *qualities through substances or elements*. For example, humours convey qualities like being good-natured or ill-tempered through substances like blood or bile. Western concepts of genetics and bodily chemistry also combine qualities and substances closely. Taking liberties with Strathern's anthropological model (for example, by locating substances as media of unmediated exchange), I would suggest that the analytical distinction between mediated and unmediated exchange can be modified to be of use to archaeologists. Unmediated exchange can be used to refer to how substances convey the transmission of qualities. In some cases the effect and 'gender' of a substance might be fixed in the material, as with Indian substance-codes where taking alcohol is absorbing heat, while in others it might still be a negotiable matter, such as the gendering of Melanesian substances. Nonetheless, substances convey qualities, and direct access to them allows the transmission of those qualities. The activation of those qualities is a contextual matter. Finally, invisible forces such as the essences of the dead or even other living people may enter into or possess the living, or take human form. Here again the whole picture is only intelligible if these forces, like 'a soul', are seen as equivalents of substances and elements and perhaps even contained within certain materials. The impossibility of finding the substance of the soul in western anatomical history means that this seems a very odd way to think to us. Yet archaeologists can, and frequently do, consider the relationship between bodies and their composite substances (e.g. flesh, blood, bone) alongside the relationship between bodies and their parts (e.g. arms, legs, head, axes). This in turn allows reflection on whether bodies could be permeated by the movement of substances or qualities alongside consideration of whether bodies and objects were made partible. In other words, it is the focus on the precise transactions and transformations themselves that allow archaeologists to frame past modes of personhood by comparison with *features* of contemporary ones. Archaeologists can therefore investigate 'economies of substances' (Thomas 1996: 164–8, and 1999b) with an eye on modes of personhood.

Substances, objects and personhood in European prehistory

A bone is an object, but bone is a substance. Animal bodies and substances (e.g. Jones 1998; Jones and Richards 2003), human bodily substances (e.g. Fowler 2001, 2002), and objects (e.g. Brück 2001a; Chapman 1996, 2000) can all be analysed as media

113

for social relations and conceptions of the world. Several of these approaches have considered the partibility of bodies. However, raw substances, including bodily substances produced by a living person, can be deployed in relations between people through either partible relations or exchanges between permeable bodies. Recently the attention of prehistorians has also shifted to consider substances in their own right, and the qualities that might be shared between substances, like colour, luminosity, durability and texture (e.g. Cummings 2002; Chapman 2002b; Fowler and Cummings 2003; Jones 2002a; Keates 2002; Parker Pearson and Ramilisonina 1998; Tilley 1996: 315–24). The biography and manipulation of substances and elements has become a vital question (e.g. Richards 1996; Thomas 1999b). The question of when a bone is an object and when it is a substance is one that can only be answered contextually, but we could start by viewing it as both. Indeed, while bodily substances like blood or milk have no given form to them, bone does: it can be measured as both substance and object. While amorphous substance can be transmitted during life, it is only after death that substances with form can be extracted from the person (see Chapman 2000: 180). Obviously any rigid distinctions would be made on cultural bases, but some materials are more ambiguous than others, with bones and fluids forming two ends of a conceptual spectrum which is more frequently a circle, since milk and semen are often thought of as forming bone. The explanation of inalienable objects already offered in Chapter 3 is that they are substitutes for the substantial relationship connecting two people. These objects do have given forms, like bones. The emphasis in Chapman's (2000) approach is on the object, rather than the substance, since objects provide the evidence for the deployment of fragmentation and curation of form that his studies reveal. Alongside this, other substances were clearly important in the southern European Neolithic and Copper Age: figurines were overwhelmingly made of brittle clay, and metals were transformed from rock ore to liquid to artefacts. Metal objects in burials were often associated with bodily orifices in the face or nether regions, or hands (Renfrew 1986: 148–9), each of which we could frame as active in exchanges.

Metals may have been luminous substance-codes that flowed and solidified like human bodily substances. They may even have moved through complementary or contrasting exchange networks to human essences. Even substances outside the body, like gold, may be absorbed into the person and/or made inalienable from social relations (see Howell 1989). For example, Keates (2002) has recently focused on the luminous nature of copper in his study of Italian Copper Age metalwork. He presents daggers as equivalents of the penis in terms of form and luminous content, and as also like bones and the radiance of the sun. The provision of the dead with daggers marked their activation as particularly luminous entities and the beginning of their transformation into the bright but numinous ancestors whose presence in the mountains was marked by stelae. These stelae were marked with depictions of daggers, including daggers placed where ribs should be, and rays of the sun. The decorated stones were frequently then 'defaced' so that they stood just as anonymous jagged lumps of ancestral substance. Clearly, metalworking in European prehistory engaged with special, luminous, transformable substances like those found within the human body and elsewhere in the cosmos. There are also other ways that substances were directed through human and non-human bodies, not least through consumption practices. For instance anthropomorphic vessels in Neolithic and Copper Age contexts in south-east Europe, such as Tisza pottery, portray the human body as a vessel into which and out of which substances may be poured. These vessels could be seen as mediators in their own right, objects as persons whose major concern was the regulation of flows of substance. The permeation of special qualities throughout the world may therefore have been manipulated through substances as well as whole and partial artefacts.

Complex artefacts combine several materials much as people do. While such objects may contain the generative qualities of those substances, they remove them from people slightly by containing them in their form. Buildings do this as well as portable artefacts. To draw on examples from the British Neolithic, contact with raw elements, including earth, fire, water, and stone, but also human remains, might be seen as having direct impact on living people. Direct engagement with water or stones might have transmitted essences between entities in a highly potent way. These were manipulated in building monuments (and thereby communities; see Barrett 1994: 29–33), putting builders in contact with special qualities (Richards 1996). Building also shaped the future transmission of qualities in those places, and regulated access to stones or chalk (see Brück 2001b). Combinations of raw materials in building monuments and making deposits throughout the period is a growing area of study (e.g. Cummings 2002; Fowler in press; Pollard 2001; Richards 1996; Thomas 1999b; cf. Owoc 2001). The key qualities contained within these substances may have been generative and transformative in nature. For example, along the Irish Sea quartz is found naturally in what were peripheral zones in the Neolithic, like beaches and mountains. On the Isle of Man quartz was frequently deposited in liminal places like causewayed enclosures (Darvill 2001) and chambered cairns (Fowler 2001, 2002, in press). Quartz was also used in building chambered cairns, particularly to mark entrances to some chambers, and contemporary quartz cairns have recently been indentified in the uplands (Davey and Woodcock in press). Pottery contained quartz inclusions (Burrow 1997). Quartz artefacts, like stone tools, were rarely made; instead, quartz was valued as a substance. Quartz perhaps simultaneously referred to substances composing the human body (bone, fat, milk, semen), and specific zones of the landscape (seashores, mountains), and may have been used to mark times for the transmission or generation of essential qualities by making the site 'wet' (Fowler in press; Fowler and Cummings 2003). These activities themselves brought the living into contact with the dead, and materials of the distant past (Fowler in press). The timing of these practices may relate to phases of the moon or even specific seasons (Darvill 2002). However, the exact manipulation of quartz would have been regarded in different ways according to gender-specific or age-specific knowledges and experiences.

Returning to the British Neolithic more generally, communal feasts such as those that took place at causewayed enclosures and later henges transmitted substances directly into the body and the impact would have been sensuous (see Hamilakis 2002). Pots as well as bodies were important mediators in these flows. For example, at the end of the Neolithic burials frequently contained decorated beakers as a standard item to which other variable assemblages might be added (Thomas 1991, and 1999a: 156–62). Beakers were sometimes buried at the foot of sarsen stones around the Avebury stone monuments, either with bodies or alone (Thomas 1999a: 218–19). Arguably, beakers were a key component of each person, a conduit for substances through the body that was usually buried when a person died. In some cases the beaker remained with the body, in others it was located in places of special potency where corpses were not admitted. Fragments of some beakers, however, were seemingly curated (see Box 3.2, pp. 72–76). Attitudes towards the bodies of the dead were also clearly different to those we have today. The bones of the dead were often successively accessed and occasionally circulated (e.g. Thomas 1999b, 2002; Fowler 2001, 2002, in press; Barrett 1988b; Richards 1988; cf. Brück 1995). Animal bones were also cached and curated (e.g. cattle skulls: Thomas 1999a: 28), and the interrelations between humans and animals were of vital importance throughout British prehistory (e.g. Ray and Thomas 2003; see Parker Pearson 1996, 1999b for Iron Age examples). Access to these remains provided intercession between the community, the ancestral dead and, arguably, generative potential. Such contact might have acted in many cases as a conduit for the transfer of energies from one part of the community to another (Barrett 1988b; Fowler in press). While human ancestral dead may be quite different from ancestral beings (Whitley 2002), it is possible that Neolithic pantheons of spirits, ancestral beings, human ancestors, animal spirits or ancestors, and so on, would have been complex and combined several groups of these entities in a holistic system of exchanges. Complex Neolithic artefacts, like hafted axes, or the bodies of people and animals, might contain a number of important essences that were shared with spiritual entities. Contextual actions, including the dismembering of bodies and breaking of objects, opened up these substances

117

to differential access and redistribution. Substances within these composite bodies may have been activated in numerous ways while intact, such as during ritual practices or in daily use. Finally, middening practices could be seen as creating homogenized pools of fertile substance-codes, generative energy accrued by the community (Fowler 2003; cf. Brück 2001a; Parker Pearson 1996: 125–7). Here bodies and things were reduced to their basic essences which coalesced over time.

While the spiritual significance of substances and the importance of symbolic conceptions of the world are illustrated here, the manipulation of substances, objects and bodies would also have been a highly political activity. There were doubtless many social agents to be consulted, listened to, and persuaded in carrying out any reconfiguration of places, things and people. In all of these cases, things, places and animals can, like people, transmit key substances and effects in both progenerative and descent relations. Their role in this process is unlikely to have been passive.

Transmission of qualities and relationships with the non-human

Not only are qualities transmitted in different ways (e.g. by descent or circulation), and through diverse media, but they may also originate from different locales. Helms (1993) has pointed out that different cultures locate the centre of the world and origin of sacred power in different places. The here and now is one locus of generation, and the distant past is an originary other (Helms 1993: 173). City-states are often lain out along the cardinal points, making the city centre the very epicentre of the cosmos, a place where different layers of reality intersect. Generative qualities emanate from this focal point. In western society, each individual is arguably presented as their own *axis mundi*, and it is within each individual that generative potential for reproduction is located. In many other societies the key energies of the cosmos are unevenly distributed among different orders of spirits, places, natural things, and kinds of people. Generative potential may be located in the past actions of ancestral entities identified with specific places and frequently encountered things, or in the continuing circulation of life-energies between beings and planes of existence. Temporary *axis mundi* may be created through the mediation of shamans and other ritual practitioners (Pentikäinen 1984). In each case, the transmission of energies is conducted through different mechanisms, and at different scales. Furthermore, different restrictions are placed on who may be included in the active transmission of knowledge and substances; in other words, who can be related to as a person and who cannot. Engagements with natural things, objects, places, and animals in the Orokaiva or 'Are'are world are engagements with spiritual entities and energies. Some of these may always be non-human, but many were once-human; even those attached to objects like axes, shell goods or personal ornaments. Some of these aspects retained the identity of what we would see as the biographical individual who owned them, but many more were anonymized powers or spirits. This section reviews cases where animals and other non-human beings are recognized as part of the community among whom substances are transmitted, and with whom relational identities are formed.

Animals and other natural things as persons: body, form and relationship

In our own society it is often difficult to tell why some animals are more like persons than others. On one level we define persons as human beings which are a species of the animal kingdom. On another level we think of ourselves as unlike other animals, although the traits we choose in making this distinction vary. Is it our self-awareness, or ability to use tools, or ability to speak, or capacity to lie, or ability to laugh, to behave morally, to interpret the world in a specific way, or our ability to adapt to all environments by using material culture (see Ingold 1988)? Many of these distinctions 'grade' animals, so some are complex and quasi-persons (e.g. an ape), while others are not (e.g. an amoeba). Some are more fully welcomed into human society (e.g. dogs) than others (e.g. foxes). However, we could say that in western conception human society exists within the natural world. As Viveiros de Castro (1996) argues, our multi-cultural world exists as a series of different cultures within a unifying human nature. In this conception, human nature is fixed and all humans share it, but we have cultural differences and we may move between cultures. Viveiros de Castro suggests that many indigenous South American societies (which he glosses as Amerindians) organize the world differently: for them, the world is multi-natural; that is, composed of beings of different natures, like tapir, jaguar or human. But all different natural species and kinds live within a single society, share a cultural world. Furthermore, just as we may move between cultures, so Amerindian people may move between natures, changing shapes. Our natural- istic multi-cultural context creates an alienating discontinuity between phenomena identified as natural versus cultural at some level. The dividing line can even exist within the person (so that some of our traits are described as natural instinct, while others are cultural). In contrast, animistic multi-natural per- spectives are founded in a continuity of relationships between all (natural and cultural) things. Whereas in our past humans descended from animals, in the Amerindian past animals were once human (particularly the dog), and are still types of people. Viveiros de Castro (1996: 473) describes a world where all rela- tions are social, and natural differences are contained within the rules of social interaction. What matters most in classifying people is what they do, what actions they engage in, what identi- ties they perform. These activities give them particular subjective positions, perspectives which are also identities (ibid.: 474). Predatory animals see humans and all other animals as prey. Prey animals see humans and other animals as predators. Because, in the human world, spirits are predators who try to kill humans, predatory animals are spirits too. The overall result is that humans and animals are all sentient beings, though some are persons and some are spirits (and potentially the spirits of the dead). Engaging with another being carries the same weight whether it is human or not; what matters is the kind of relation- ship between the beings involved, such as whether they are

animism

predator and prey. Thinking from the other's point of view is part of the relationship between humans and non-humans, and all beings may exchange perspectives with one another. It is also notable that humans, particularly shamans, can become animals and that predatory animal spirits can take human forms. As Viveiros de Castro explains, all beings share the same type of spirit, but their bodies vary. Changing the appearance of the body therefore makes a statement about relationships, moving human beings from one 'nature' or kind to another. Qualities like the spirit are extended to the animals and can in fact be more basic features of the world than mutable physical bodies. Natural places are often thought of as places built by animals; for example, a watering hole where tapir gather is thought of as the ceremonial house of the tapir people. Animals, objects, buildings, places and even unseen forces like spirits that lack bodies or live in mythical creatures can all be persons. These spiritual entities influence and even become part of a person, and in some cases can take human form, or will possess the bodies of living people. This is not unintelligible to us, but while we might recognize similarities between humans, animals and objects (all are composites with biographies), we might find it harder to see natural objects as persons. However this distinction between natural and cultural objects is not commonly made outside the west. Morris notes that the Ojibwa categorize some things as just inanimate things, while

> certain classes of objects, certain shells or stones, may under specific circumstances be considered animate, while such natural phenomena as thunder, sun and moon . . . are thought of not only as animate by the Ojibwa, but as categorised as persons.
>
> (Morris 1994: 9)

Ojibwa interactions with worldly things depend on whether they are classified as inanimate objects, animate objects, or persons (see Howell 1996). What can different ways of relating to natural phenomena, animals, objects, plants and places tell us about personhood?

Naturalism, totemism and animism

Viveiros de Castro makes a distinction between our own naturalistic society and animistic societies. This stems from Descola's (1996) description of three *modes of identification*, and has also influenced Ingold's analysis of totemic and animistic ways of being. According to Ingold (2000b) there is a fundamental distinction between human relationships with the world which are totemic and those which are animistic. The basic difference is the way that human beings identify themselves in comparison to animals and the other entities with whom they share the world. Totemic relations are connections with places containing ancestral energies. The ancestry of humans and certain animals can both be traced from the land, and so they each contain the same energies associated with specific places, specific ancestral beings (Ingold 2000b: 113). Ingold argues that totemic relations stress the replication of past practices and material forms in maintaining a flow of ancestral substance from generation to generation. Here the land and specific *places*, rather than the animals or other entities, are of the utmost importance since they embody the essential tie between all beings. These beings are dividual and share some of the same ancestral substances in their composition. Animistic relations, on the other hand, take the form of negotiations with *all* kinds of entities. These are seen as social peers, and fully relational interactions take place between these beings (Bird-David 1993, 1999). Humans are within the world with these other beings, and attempt to understand things from perspectives other than their own; from the perspective of these other entities (e.g. Ingold 2000d). The forms beings take depend on their relations with others (Ingold 2000d: 109). These interactions do not end with the death of any being, and may include the manipulation of human and animal body parts. There are prescribed ways that the components of dead bodies must be treated to ensure the continued transmission of essences. Among many northern Eurasian animic communities this includes the proper sharing and disposal of body parts after a kill, necessary for the reproduction of that animal species (Ingold 1986: 246–7). Physical partibility is one mechanism of the dividuality present in animic systems. Shamans are often necessary mediators with the animal and spiritual world, since hunting and other interactions with these beings may be draining to human beings – shamans reclaim the lost energies and even lost souls from the otherworld (Ingold 1986: 247, and 2000b: 115). In totemic systems spiritual qualities are, however, fairly fixed in the body, so there is no need for shamanic mediation between humans and other entities (Ingold 2000b: 115). While shamans leave the body to engage with animal spirits, the totemic person has a part of the animal within him or her already, and vice versa: they share substance. However, the butchery and sharing of animals in totemic systems also involves the redistribution of substance, but this focuses on kinship relations in the community (ibid.: 117–19). The redistribution is not in itself generative of more animals, and the hunt is not a dialogue with animals so much as a commemorative movement around the ancestral landscape.

I have summarised an interpretation of totemism, animism and naturalism in Table 5.1. However, following Lévi-Strauss's analysis of totemism as an uncritical agglomeration of different systems (Lévi-Strauss 1964), Descola and Viveiros de Castro define totemic systems as those classifications which use natural emblems only as *symbols* of a relationship (e.g. to delineate one group of people as eagles in relation to another group as crows). Descola and Viveiros de Castro are therefore more concerned with the distinctions between animism (a multi-natural social world) and naturalism (a multi-cultural natural world). Vitally, however, Descola (1996: 88) points out that no community need be only animistic or totemic, and *these ways of relating are not mutually exclusive*. Some societies therefore combine degrees of both these analytical constructs.

Naturalism, animism and totemism provide frames of reference for thinking about the situation of human persons alongside

Table 5.1 Totemism, animism and naturalism (based on interpretation of Descola 1996, Ingold 2000b and Viveiros de Castro 1996)

	Animism (Viveiros de Castro, Descola, Ingold, and Bird-David)	Totemism (according to Ingold)	Naturalism (Descola, Viveiros de Castro)
The nature of identity	Status of beings is negotiable; the relation between people, animals and things is dialogic	Animals, people and things are essentially 'what they are' but can communicate with one another	Identity is fixed by species
Life energies	No fixed source of life energy; energy is circulated and generated through relationships	Ancestors are the source of energy and shaped the form of the world. Living beings gain their energy from the land	Life as an energy comes from God, nature or biochemical processes
The transmission of form	Transformation of forms is vital to interaction between beings – each takes on a form appropriate to the relationship they are currently engaged in	Maintenance of forms through the faithful reproduction of traditional practices, and above all the custodianship of the land, is vital to ensuring the transmission of energies to living things	Forms are reproduced identically by natural reproduction from one generation to another

Sense of community	Non-human persons are part of the human social world: nature is society, and species constitute different social groups. However, species may appear in forms that are not their own.	Human persons along with other beings live together in the land, which is the trace of ancestral presence. Human society draws on natural forms for making social distinctions	The human world *is* the social world, and human society or culture is a part of nature
The attainment of personhood	Animals, objects, places and plants can all potentially be persons, and parts of persons	Animals, objects, places and plants are *like* persons, and share ancestral energies with persons through their shared connection to place and descent from the ancestral being of that place	Only human beings can be fully persons; and animals, objects, places and plants can only be thought of as persons in whimsical or fantastic contexts. Any metaphor between human and non-human is thought to be simply representational

others within the world. These heuristics illustrate that in many cases society and community are far more extensive than common western conception allows. These relations cut to the heart of personhood. For example, prehistoric people may have included animals within their communities, and even within their descent group (Jones and Richards 2003; Ray and Thomas 2003). Like human people, animals might have been dividual persons, shaped through contextually specific trends in partibility or permeability, rather than indivisible entities isolated from the community at large and thought of as resources. Thinking about animals in this way provides a useful perspective on prehistoric butchery, consumption preferences, daily routines with livestock or prey, and depositional practices. Contact with the bones of dead animals alongside dead humans was clearly an important feature of the British Neolithic, for instance, suggesting an equivalence of one kind or another (e.g. Jones 1998; Whittle *et al.* 1998). The role of animal bodies and their partibility will be revisited through a case study in Chapter 6.

Predation, protection and reciprocity: attitudes towards others and means of acquiring substance

Descola (1996) outlines predation, protection and reciprocity as different modes of relations which intersect with his modes of identification. These modes of relations describe the attitude with which humans engage with the non-human world: by violently extracting from it (predation); by conserving and maintaining it (protection); and by engaging with it in a mutually interactive way (reciprocity). Attitudes do not mesh directly with means of subsistence: while subsistence practices may include hunting the relation between those people and animals may still be one of either shared descent (protection) or respectful co-existence (reciprocity) rather than vengeful action or detached slaughter (predation). Susan Kent (1989) has argued that societies which hunt for food see prey animals as sentient, while societies which keep domesticated animals see them as dumb. But, as Ingold (1994, 1996) warns, we cannot presume that past societies

126

saw agricultural practices as exploitative and domestic animals as dumb – as we have seen, domestic pigs in Melanesia may be persons.

Attitudes describe relations with the whole world, and archaeologists are only be able to postulate such attitudes through close contextual analysis stretching well beyond subsistence practices. Human relations with each other also potentially operate through the same modes – Descola stresses the role of predatory relations in Amerindian exchanges. Here marriage, death, food procurement, and all other exchanges are predominantly predatory in nature. Palsson (1996) suggests three attitudes isomorphic to Descola's: orientalism, paternalism and communalism. These are evident in human relations with the environment at large. Orientalism is identified as domination over the natural world, an exploitative relation, paternalism is founded in the protection and curation of the world, and a (delayed) reciprocal relation between the environment and people, while communalism is founded in a continual dialogic co-existence with the world. Each of these relations applies to human encounters with the environment in Palsson's account, but could also equally apply to human interactions with each other. Palsson's discussion of Icelandic fishing practices illustrates that there may be no clear-cut affinity between attitudes and modes of identification at all. The Icelandic fishermen exist in a modern naturalist society, and were primarily of a predatory attitude towards the sea until the Cod Wars and decline of the fish population. Co-operation with environmentalists and government agencies changed their attitudes to a more protective relationship, and even into an ecologically concerned reciprocal relationship. What this may suggest is that, in the same way that the individual facet of the person is predominant but not all-pervasive in modernity, so predatory action may be predominant but not all-encompassing in naturalistic contexts. Once again we are required to acknowledge certain degrees of cultural tendencies rather than absolute distinctions. However, attitudes towards the world may be archaeologically visible in human engagement with the environment, and may also reveal the kinds of relationships that shape personhood, the kinds of interactions and transactions between people. While dominant social attitudes will be very difficult to detect archaeologically, the degree and nature of inter-personal violence, the nature of subsistence strategies and cycles of land use might all be useful starting points. Exactly how substances are extracted and circulated is therefore not only a matter of social strategy but of cultural attitude. Signs of violence in prehistory may not relate only to conflict between communities, but also to the motivating concerns in how personhood was attained, and how relations with certain kinds of people were predominantly negotiated.

Conclusion

In the world of the indivisible person substances and properties are contained within the individual and within things. The two do not interpenetrate one another in common conception. However, dividuals may be interpenetrated continually by flows of substance and vital essences. Dividual people redirect these flows in knowledgeable ways, anticipating changing relationships – not just with other humans but with non-human dividuals. Non-human bodies like houses or pots may not be representations of human bodies, but may instead be the fractal bodies of non-human persons at different scales. This can apply equally to animals, monuments and even entire landscapes. All of these bodies are produced through social activity, and are multiply-authored. Continuous processes of transformation are visited upon all of these bodies. Therefore, studies of personhood are concerned with the way the materiality of the whole cosmos is managed, not just the individual body. It makes a great deal of difference whether archaeologists imagine past people interacting with animals, rocks, and objects as people, or as just exploiting resources. In studying prehistory it is vital to bear in mind that different concepts of personhood would have involved radically different understandings of and engagements with the material world to those we expect today.

In the past four chapters several affiliated concepts have been developed. Three trends in the principles that give shape to relationships have been discussed, each of which supports articulation of the fixed (individual) and relational (dividual) aspects of the person in different ways. These are indivisible individuality, partibility modulating with dividuality, and permeability. Derived from Melanesian ethnography, partibility has been reframed here as a term applicable to relations of personhood in other contexts. Derived from Indian ethnography, permeability has the potential to describe bounded people who are permeable to the essences of the world. Two different modes of generation have also been explored, one predicated on passing generative potential on through descent, the other on the knowledgeable ongoing and open circulation of substances, which are also erstwhile parts of people, in a progenerative process. In its most extreme incarnation the first of these supports indivisible personhood, but most communities operate a mixture of both. The second 'rhizomic' pattern strongly suggests dividuality in either partible or permeable modes. Modes of identification have also been introduced to describe trends in relationships between the human and non-human as animic/animistic, totemic or naturalistic. Both animism and totemism entail fractal and dividual personhood, but in different ways. Animism in particular involves highly relational personhood, including open negotiation with non-human persons. Finally, interactions between entities are carried out within particular attitudes. In fully relational personhood, where animals, plants and rocks might be people, we would expect very similar attitudes to extend to interactions with all these people. All of these heuristics will be drawn on in describing a mode of personhood through an extended case study in Chapter 6.

6

PERSONHOOD IN LATER MESOLITHIC SCANDINAVIA

An interpretation

Introduction

This chapter offers an interpretation of personhood in Mesolithic southern Scandinavia between around 5400 and 4600 BC, weaving together the threads teased out in previous chapters.

Setting the scene

Locating the Ertebølle

The earlier part of the Ertebølle period, 5400–4600 BC was aceramic, and is famous for its burials. Inland campsites have provided evidence of fur trapping and hunting, as at Ringkloster, and shell middens accumulated at coastal gathering places, as at Bjørnsholm and Ertebølle (Figure 6.1). People probably moved between these different locales on a seasonal round fluctuating between temporary campsites and longer-term coastal settlements, making use of a wide range of animals and plants. Stable isotope analysis and archaeological remains suggest that the main food source was seafood; fish, eels and shellfish. At the same time inland camps like Ringkloster contained the stripped carcasses of pine martens, polecats and other small fur-bearing animals. The archaeological record from throughout Mesolithic Denmark is very rich (for related in-depth studies, see Strassburg 2000; Tilley 1996), and submerged sites have yielded wood and fibre

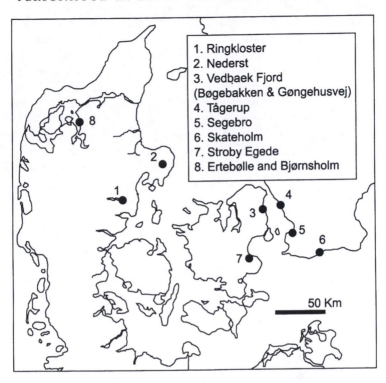

1. Ringkloster
2. Nederst
3. Vedbaek Fjord
   (Bøgebakken & Gøngehusvej)
4. Tågerup
5. Segebro
6. Skateholm
7. Stroby Egede
8. Ertebølle and Bjørnsholm

50 Km

Figure 6.1 Map of key Mesolithic sites in southern Scandinavia.

remains. Decorated paddles, long hollow-log canoes, bows and arrows, fishing spears, weirs and fish-traps have all been found. Axes were made from or hafted with antler, and a whole variety of tools were made from animal bones and antler. From 4600 BC pottery was made, and bone ornaments included, in the western regions, polished arm-rings from the shoulder blades of aurochs and other large mammals.

The bodies and persons discussed here are those of the earlier, aceramic Ertebølle. There are two main cemeteries at Skateholm, Scania, one dating to around 5400–4900 BC, the other to 5400–4600 BC (Larsson 1988, 1989a, 1989b, 1993). Skateholm II is the earliest and Skateholm I the latest. Most segments of human

131

society are well-represented at both sites: young and old, male and female are all present. There was also a mixture of human and animal bodies; of 77 burials found in both sites ten were single burials of dogs and seven human burials also contained the remains of dogs. The cemetery at Vedbaek Bøgebakken (henceforth Vedbaek) is just on the other side of the Øresund, on the east coast of Zealand (Albrethsen and Brinch Petersen 1976). It is very similar to Skateholm: a coastal cemetery, with a poorly preserved settlement, and dates to roughly the same period, *c.* 5400–4700 BC. Although not fully preserved it contained at least 22 bodies. Most of the graves contained similar grave goods, and corpses were frequently dressed with ochre. Layers of occupational debris were also found at Vedbaek, showing intensive exploitation of seal, wild pig, deer, water-birds and fish. There are several other burial groups or cemeteries from this period, including those from sites at Tågerup, Segebro, Gøngehusvej and Nederst (Figure 6.1). Each of these sites include areas of occupation or gathering activity, and human and dog burials.

Mortuary practices as transformations

Some of the Ertebølle dead were buried in cemeteries, some under dwellings, some in more isolated locales, some were cremated (Brinch Petersen and MeikleJohn 2003), and some were pushed out to sea or tethered to the shore in boats (Grøn and Skaarup 1991). These latter activities transformed and 'moved' the dead, started them off on a journey. Cemeteries seem to be deliberately located near to the heads of rivers and fjords, and these locales had a persistent history of use even though rising sea levels sometimes encroached on the existing cemeteries and occupation areas. The dead were transformed within a liminal zone where land, sea and sky met. Cremations send smoke up into the sky and disperse the parts of the person, often in a violent and memorable transformation that causes the bodies of the dead to tense, convulse, sit up or even explode (H. Williams in press). Strassburg (2000: 180–2) suggests that other mortuary practices anchored the dead bodies firmly in place – several were pinned down in their graves with

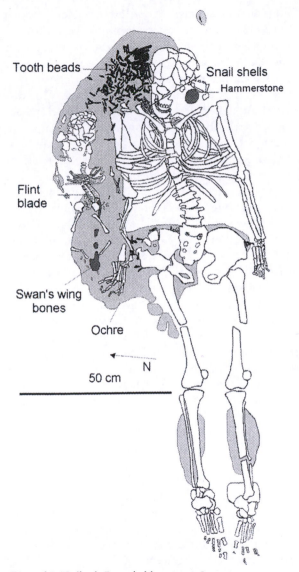

Figure 6.2 Vedbaek Bøggebakken grave 8.
Source: Adapted from Albrethsen and Brinch Petersen (1976).

large stones (e.g. Vedbaek grave 10; Albrethsen and Brinch Petersen 1976: 12–13). A wide variety in mortuary practice is evident, including cases of exhumation and secondary use or burial of remains. Decisions as to which set of practices to apply may have been based on multiple highly contingent criteria.

Bodies were placed in graves either wrapped in hides, or displaying collections of material culture about them. However, the artefacts found with the inhumations and the cremations should not be seen solely as direct indicators of the individual lives of the deceased even if they were used to cite social relationships: several infants and even a dog were provided with tools. The burials are of largely intact human bodies, some containing two, three or more humans (Figure 0.1), and some a human and a dog. For example, grave 8 at Vedbaek contained one 18-year-old female and a newly born baby (Figure 6.2; Albrethsen and Brinch Peterson 1976: 10–11). There were 190 beads or pendants made from drilled red deer and wild boar teeth, and a lump of perforated snail shells was placed next to the adult's skull. A similar collection of snail shells was found curled up under her pelvis alongside teeth from deer, seals and elk. A hammer-stone lay near the other side of the adult's head. The baby lay to one side, near the shoulder of the woman, and rested on a swan's wing. The body was covered in ochre and a truncated flint blade lay in its lap. One deposit at Gøngehusvej 7 contained the remains of five cremated bodies, seemingly in various states of decay when they were burnt (Brinch Petersen and MeikleJohn 2003). These multiple burials can be explained in many ways, but Zvelebil (1997) recounts how those who die in winter in parts of Siberia are left in platforms suspended in trees until the annual gathering where all that year's dead will be buried together: we can postulate a communal mortuary gathering. Gøngehusvej 7 deposit N seems to consist of the remains of just such a collective pyre during an annual gathering. The dead, dressed and decorated, may have been on display during extended mortuary cycles or during a brief period before interment. However, Nilsson Stutz (2003) notes that corpses were not in advanced states of decay when interred, and graves were backfilled immediately. Some of the grave fills contain fragmented objects and what appear to be the remains of meals (e.g. Larsson 1989b: 373; Strassburg 2000: 169–70). There is only one case of disarticulation of a fresh corpse at either Skateholm or Vedbaek – one hand and foot were missing from the heap of remains in grave 13 at Skateholm I that were dismembered while still fleshed. Grave 28 had been partly reopened and some bones removed during advanced stages of decay or later. There is evidence that a few skulls were cut from corpses at Dyrholmen, Jutland and defleshed (Tilley 1996: 43). Human remains have been found among other highly fragmented occupation waste, including two human bones in Vedbaek occupational material, and disarticulated 'relic' human bones have been recovered along with the corpses at Stroby Egede (Strassburg 2000: 225), and in midden deposits (Tilley 1996: 43). While the presence of these fragmented remains appears unusual, burial itself was by no means extended to all members of society. Body parts from the majority of the dead may themselves have been dispersed, circulated, or deposited in other locales. The beginnings of what would in later periods be seen as structured deposition (e.g. at Ringkloster and at Gøngehusvej 7: Andersen 1995; Brinch Petersen and MeikleJohn 2003) also suggests that the retention of animal body parts was important, and that the deposition of humans and animals might be thought of in equivalent ways. As we have seen, mortuary practice can in some cases be thought of as a kind of exchange or even sacrifice; one element in a holistic system of exchanges. Each mortuary practice was probably a transformation of the person, affecting both the dead and the living.

Material culture and body parts

Specific animal body parts were used to ornament the dead human body. Ducks' feet, the beaks of water birds, and birds' wings – a swan at Vedbaek, a bird of the crow family at Nederst – sharks' teeth, boars' tusks, brown bear bones, claws and teeth, wolves' teeth, red deer, roe deer, dog, elk, wild boar and auroch teeth were all buried attached to or associated with the human body in these graves. Tooth beads sometimes included human teeth: three perforated human teeth were part of a chain of around fifty found in Vedbaek grave 19c. The jaws of pine martens and other small fur-bearing animals were sometimes placed on the bodies of the dead. Deer hooves were also interred with the dead, in some cases possibly indicating the presence of animal hides; but animal feet also seem to have been of interest in themselves. Detailed taphonomic studies of graves XV and X at Skateholm II indicate that the bodies were tightly bound up or wrapped before burial, and that the necklaces, tools, weapons and other ornaments were bound intimately to the body within these wrappings (Nilsson 1998). Fragmented animal body parts were associated with specific parts of integral human bodies: teeth and jaws were often worn about the head and chest, perhaps valorizing those parts of the human body associated with consumption. Perforated tooth beads were common, in strings of varying lengths. Teeth were also grouped in what we could refer to as display cloths or panels, and these were sometimes laid over or under the waist. These need not necessarily have been worn as garments, though this is a possibility, but they were placed over certain bodily orifices. These could be thought of as entry points through which the body could be altered or could affect other bodies (cf. Strassburg 2000: 196). The mouth, for example is the conduit of speech, communication, consumption, of breath and also often the spirit. Jaws and teeth form the physical remains of the mouth. Animal jaws are commonly found on the head, throat or chest of the dead, areas perhaps associated with breath, consumption, speech and life (ibid.). Feet are associated with movement, as are wings used to leave the ground and fly into the air. The feet, claws and wings of animals referred to patterns in ways that animals moved, or interactions in ways that emulated those animals. Water-birds could exist on land, in the sea, and in the sky, moving through all spheres of the cosmos (ibid.: 185). Antler axes and antler biers were made from the *exuviae* of animals – things which could be shed and could be used by humans while the animal was still alive, and which would be renewed every year. Although we cannot find furs, we can infer that animal fur was a vital part of Ertebølle dress. Animal body parts utilized were in many cases the parts of animals which were instrumental in their relations with human beings and one another – the things they used to flee from or to fight other beings with. These animal body parts may also have conferred animal-like qualities into the person wearing them. Not just animals, but also the elements of the world itself were invoked in the transformation of the dead. Ochre was clearly an important symbolic media which both coloured the bodies of dead persons and connected them with the substance of the land. This transformed and may have preserved the appearance of dead temporarily. Objects crafted from antler were reductions from a single branch of substance, and as such might have been bonded to the other artefacts made from the same piece of antler – there are distinct possibilities for partible objects emergent from shared origins. Antler might be amorphous and dividual into many artefacts in its raw state: while it has a form of its own that form was made partible in artefact production. Stone artefacts may also have incorporated a diversity of worldly parts and essences into the person. Any of these objects might have become persons and/or part of persons, and mediated in social relations with other beings including plants and prey (cf. Strassburg 2000: 97–8).

Tracing relations

Composite objects and reconfigured relationships

As well as partible objects produced through reductive or extractive techniques, there were composite objects, which we could see as multiply-authored by members of the human and non-human community, including the animals that many of them were extracted from (see Finlay 2003). Chains of relations were perhaps traced through the acquisition, fashioning, exchange and curation of tooth beads, particularly if those animals had spiritual significance. These necklaces, strings and panels were superlative composite items, and each tooth had been part of an original set, then broken up and redistributed. Each string was the product of many transactions with animals and between humans, not least in the hunt. Several burials contain a few beads or only single beads, while a few contain almost complete sets of teeth from one jaw (see below). Across the main aceramic Ertebølle burial sites 44 per cent of all tooth ornaments were associated with women, 17 per cent with adult males, and the rest with children or unidentifiable remains (see Knutsson 2000: 30, but cf. Schmidt in press). The most numerous tooth beads at Vedbaek were associated with one body within double or triple burials. Perhaps in these cases such beads could not be passed along the relationship between the people interred, or perhaps a collective burial involved offering a composite artefact.

Necklaces, bracelets and other strings of beads as well as single beads have been found in other contexts. While some were buried or burnt with the dead, others were kept among the living community; only 18 per cent of burials at Vedbaek included tooth beads. Teeth have also been found as 'stray finds' or among occupation debris (e.g. the lower front jaw set from a red deer found at Bjørnsholm: Andersen 1991: 83–4, fig. 23), and necklaces have been found deposited in campsites and lakes (Strassburg 2000: 279). As well as being composite objects, necklaces could also potentially be taken to pieces. Other beads from the same original chains were perhaps redistributed in making new necklaces, and new chains of relations. Strings of teeth sometimes included those from elk or aurochs, animals which were rare or absent in the area around Vedbaek and Skateholm at the time. These may have been valued exchange items. The teeth from rare or perhaps extinct animals may have been curated items, and it has also been argued that some of the decorated objects in some Ertebølle graves were older curated items (e.g. Nash 1998: 13). These kinds of objects formed connections with the past through animal body matter. Like the bodies of the dead these artefacts belonged to and were inalienable from the community. Collectively, the social body was reworked every time a member of the community was made partible from it and buried. Different parts of the collective person were redistributed and reconfigured during mortuary gatherings, feasts, and possibly exchanges. A wide variety of relations were traced through curated animal teeth, human teeth, and other human and non-human body parts or substances, unravelling a complex narrative of transactions that assembled new collectives out of older elements. Not all of these activities focused on corpses, though the body was clearly a vital conduit through which relations were monitored. While the removal of bones and fresh limbs was rare, it was practised, and cremation deposits are rather partial, leaving open the possibility that some elements of the person were physically relocated. Although the 40 graves at Skateholm I were well-spaced, some were cut into by later graves, perhaps deliberately adding the body of one person to the remains of another (e.g. graves 46 and 47). Past relations could perhaps be revisited through a variety of material means.

Paths, tasks and places

The animal body parts chosen to adorn many of the human bodies also traced connections to specific locales or ecological zones. Some animals, like water-birds, may have been particularly valued because they moved between these zones. Pine marten are tree-climbers, at home on land, are excellent swimmers, and are active at night. Water snail shells were also used as beads, perhaps tracing a connection with a specific micro-environment, and fish were commonly found in graves (Jonsson 1986). A bog at Ageröd, Scania, has yielded a necklace of hazelnuts (Larsson 1983: 72), suggesting that strings of other perishable materials have been lost in mortuary contexts. Nuts from one tree could form a natural set, like a human community. Different tree species may have been used in different practices. Wooden artefacts were placed in graves, including from trays and possibly coffins, though Nilsson Stutz (2003) has argued that remains of wood from some Skateholm I graves were not from coffins. Oak was used to cremate the dead in Gønghusvej 7 deposit N, while apple was more frequently used in hearths.

Animal species (as well as plants, trees and minerals) are a major feature in the identity of specific places (Jones 1998). The body parts chosen for association with humans, like wings, were the most distinctive features of how each animal engaged with its environment and with other animals. Jaws, beaks and teeth denoted what each animal ate, and whether it hunted, scavenged or grazed. Animal and human biographies were intertwined. The consumption of particular foods and engagement in practices like hunting, trapping, fur and hide preparation, shellfish gathering, or fishing identified both places and participants. The tools buried with the dead stressed the importance of such daily tasks in locating the deceased among wider society, and qualifying them as members of the community, *whether they had used those tools in life or not*. The burial of infant and dog bodies with tools suggests that burials did not necessarily reflect what we would see as the real biographies of dead individuals, and may have provided subject positions for them, making them into certain kinds of person. The provision of knives in particular afforded them the ability to cut, to apportion food or to sever and reconnect social relations. The location of knives near to the umbilical region may also have been of significance. Williams's (2002) description of knives with souls accompanying dead animals also springs to mind. However, we could argue that the dead were provided with the opportunity to mimic the activities of living humans, just as provision with animal body parts may have allowed them to move and interact like living animals. Providing relational positions for the dead illustrates the way that these bodies belonged to the community and were continually recreated through mutual social interaction. The burial of the dead in special locales, and with material references to particular tasks, could also be seen as mediation between the living community and that of the dead and also animals. These deposits may have relocated the person in the cosmos by projecting them into certain relationships and perspectives, and/or have been intended to move and transform an aspect of the dead person, like a spirit. As we will see they might also have been important ways to return essences to the cosmos and ensure the renewal of herds of deer and schools of fish.

Campsites were also places where animal bodies were transformed, perhaps alongside the transformation and decoration of the human body. The gathering of materials, including those from animal bodies, to nourish and transform the appearance of human bodies was arguably a driving force at many of these sites. Preferences for capturing particular species (e.g. white-tailed eagles at Øgårde: Grigson 1989) also suggests that the identity of each place might be bound up in the kinds of animals killed there. Campsites, therefore, may have been important places of transformation for a host of bodies and forms, and locales for the commemoration and regeneration of those bodies. A combination of the theoretical approaches discussed so far and some ethnographic analogies provides a closer reading of the connections between people, animals and landscape, and the practices core to the modes of personhood in these communities.

Closer interpretations? Analogy, context and the direct historical approach

Zvelebil (1997, 2003) offers an ethnographic analogy with the western Siberian Kets as an example of a northern Eurasian cosmology shared by fisher-forager-hunters, and suggests a direct historical connection between these communities and those of prehistoric northern Eurasia. Within this cosmology persons are composed of three aspects – the physical body, the body-soul and the free-soul. We tend to think of people as having a single, indivisible soul since we conceptualize the person as indivisible. However, the body-soul in particular is 'almost infinitely divisible', each part of the body having its own portion of soul, and 'any of these bits may inadvertently be mislaid or stolen' (Ingold 1986: 246). Humans, bears and elk are comparable in possessing these attributes (shamans in particular can move between these three forms). The free-souls of most fur-bearing animals, fish and birds reside collectively in a spiritual being referred to as the animal master. They are only manifestations of the animal master. It is the animal master who must be engaged with dialogically when interacting with any member of the species. Domestic animals have no free-souls since their agency is subject to human action: in effect, humans become their animal masters

(Ingold 1986: 272–3). All animals have a body-soul which resides in the components of their bodies. The spiritual elements of both humans and animals are therefore distributed through the world, and their condensation in one body can be a tenuous situation to maintain. Ingold comments that:

> the hunter lives by killing and eating animals, which inevitably involves their dismemberment. Much of the ritual surrounding the treatment of slaughtered beasts, particularly concerning the preservation of bones and other inedible parts, and their deposition in the correct medium and precise order that they occur in the skeleton, is designed to assist the reconstitution of the animals from the pieces into which they have been broken for the purposes of consumption, thus ensuring the regeneration of that on which human life depends . . . human beings, too are fragile and temporary constructions that can all too easily fall apart . . .
>
> (Ingold 1986: 246–7)

Killing an animal is part of a sacrificial act, opening up the possibility of cosmological renewal and regeneration, proving that the extracted part of the world is properly divided up, and provided that the parts are shared appropriately among the community (Ingold 1986: ch. 10). Following a kill a hunter shares the parts of the carcass with others, returning substance to the community at large, since it has been killed on behalf of the community (Ingold 1986: 227). We could argue that the social redistribution of joints of meat involves the extraction of a part of the person since they have incorporated the animal body by taking it from its animal master. Giving this part away fulfils a debt both to other humans in the community, and also to the animal world and cosmos at large. Killing is necessary for regeneration (Ingold 1986: 250).

The cosmos of these northern Eurasian communities is tripartite, with the earth in the centre above a lower inverted world of the dead and beneath an upper world of the sky (Ingold

1986: 246; Zvelebil 1997). Fish and water-birds mediate the transitions between these worlds, and watery places are particularly significant points of intersection between the worlds of the living and the dead. Free-souls are sometimes conceptualized as a bird, or a shadow that can fly away from the body (Lopatin 1960: 28–34). A cosmic river runs between the worlds, also conceptualized vertically as a tree or a pillar. Shamans move along these axes between worlds, and are important social negotiators between them. Zvelebil's (1997) account of Ket landscape use integrates a holistic social cycle of seasonal mobility and subsistence economy along rivers with this cosmology and ritual activity.

Several features suggest an appropriate comparison with the southern Scandinavian Mesolithic. These include the likelihood of seasonal mobility patterns along waterways to the coast, social aggregation at the heads of rivers and fjords, the decline in the richness of grave goods towards old age, and a symbolic emphasis on deer, bear, fish and water-birds. It has also been argued that the division of the cosmos into an underworld, the earth, and the upper world was a common theme in northern European mythology, including during the Scandinavian Bronze and Iron Ages (e.g. Bradley 2000: 142–3; Parker Pearson 1999a: 70; M. Williams 2001). Depictions of body parts like limbs appear alongside whole human and animal bodies in Scandinavian rock art from different periods (e.g. Yates 1993). General analogies about circumpolar cosmologies are appealing to some degree in interpreting the prehistory of the far north of Europe, and Zvelebil's interpretation of the far earlier site of Oleneostrovski mogilnik is effective, but interpretations based on these ethnographies often tend to focus heavily on shamans. Other members of society also engaged with the world through the same structuring principles and conceptions of personhood. It is not only shamans who engage with powerful animals on a regular basis, though they may seek to help recover parts of persons lost in such encounters. Strassburg's interpretation (2000) also rejects a simple reading of individual status and recognises substances and fragmented body parts as significant individual relations. However, he argues that burial dealt correctively with dangerous or 'queer' individuals, like shamans. My account does not exclude the possible presence of Mesolithic shamans and a cosmology related to or analogous to recent northern Eurasian ones (cf. Schmidt 2000). It considers what can be said about personhood more broadly in a world of fully dialogic relations understood through the conceptual schemes outlined in previous chapters.

Patterns in Ertebølle personhood

Humans and animals

At some point during dressing, wrapping and burial, ochre was often used to colour the assembled human corpse. Polished bone and flint tools were held or worn, and beads were sometimes present in their hundreds. The effect of these displays could be quite dazzling, demonstrating that the person was composed from a diversity of relationships with animals, places and other human beings. Each was therefore presented as a fractal composite of relations, drawing together the whole community and cosmos in their person. But how were animals rendered after death?

Dogs were ambiguous entities in the Mesolithic world. They were domesticated and lived among human society, but were also mediators in the hunting and killing of other animals for humans (Tilley 1996: 65). They could sense the world in a way people could not, with heightened olfactory and auditory senses. Dogs (or at the very least their teeth) were sometimes exchanged over long distances in the Baltic Mesolithic (Eriksson and Zagorska 2003). Among animal species, only the bodies of dogs were buried whole like humans or alongside humans (the roe deer fawn placed over a cremation at Gøngehusvej 7 providing an interesting exception: Brinch Petersen and MeikleJohn 2003: 489). Out of 77 graves at Skateholm I and II, 17 were of dogs or included dogs alongside humans. Several dogs were buried in their own graves, and some contained comparatively rich grave goods. One dog burial, grave XXI in Skateholm II, was the most lavishly treated of all the graves (Figure 6.3). The dog was laid on its left side, crouched:

A red deer antler was laid along its spine and three flint blades were placed in the hip region, in precisely the same fashion as that in which such objects appear in male human graves . . . a decorated antler hammer was laid on the dog's chest.

(Larsson 1993: 53)

Few humans were given such treatment, and many human adults had no grave goods. Like humans, dogs could be buried with many grave goods, or none, and were frequently strewn with ochre. Most dogs were buried in a crouched position, a practice that was eventually extended to humans at Skateholm I, particularly women. However, dogs were *not* associated with the teeth of other animals, and in Skateholm I most of the dog burials were

Figure 6.3 Grave XXI, Skateholm II.

Source: Larsson (1989a). Reprinted by kind permission of Lars Larsson.

placed slightly apart from the human burials (Larsson 1990: 155–6). Both dogs and humans were sometimes killed in violent ways. Dogs were often decapitated and either the skull or body, or both, were interred in graves on their own or with humans, as in grave XIII, Skateholm II, where a large decapitated dog lay over the legs of a woman (Larsson 1989a, 1990). Some humans displayed signs of violence, including arrowheads lodged in bones (e.g. Grave 19a). Grave 33, Skateholm I, contained another adult male who had a cracked but healed skull – at least three burials in Skateholm I exhibited this sign of violence (Strassburg 2000: 163). The male in grave 33, had also suffered from an injured right knee. The body had been thrown in head first and arrows were shot into the grave (ibid.). Corpses in many Ertebølle burials had been shot, though it is not possible to tell whether this was a cause of death or a post-mortem ritualized killing of the corpse. A dog's skull was placed over grave 33, along with bone fragments and flints. While in some cases dogs were dismembered or not interred intact in what we would see as mortuary contexts, the same is true for some humans who were partially dismembered, while others were presumably not buried at all.

There were some limits to the similarities between dogs and humans, but we could certainly see some dogs as emergent persons, as Lars Larsson has argued (Larsson 1989a, 1990). We could see dogs as encapsulated by single people and perhaps the community, the collective person. Social activities like hunting, or guarding the young, revealed each dog's own cultural dispositions and attitudes, their membership of the community. In contemporary ethnographies of northern Eurasian peoples, dogs fall into the class of domestic animals, which have no free-soul; 'the spirit of the domestic animal is the soul of man, controlling the animal from without' (Ingold 1986: 255). Dogs are commonly used as sacrifices among these communities, and the violent treatment of some Ertebølle dogs could be seen in that light. In effect the dog was a part of the person, encapsulated by them: sacrificing a dog would be to offer up a part of the person and community.

Human connections with other animals were rather different. Several contrasting strategies of fragmentation and association are evident in the generation of relations across species. Humans were often buried intact in the skins of animals, while pine marten were skinned and their otherwise intact bodies discarded. Such skinned bodies were found in the lake by the campsite at Ringkloster (Andersen 1995: 51). The pelvis was marked out as a zone of deposition for some human burials, while at Ringkloster seven deer pelvises were deposited in a stack (ibid.: 28). Almost all species could be hunted, killed, eaten, buried whole, or fragmented and redistributed in either analogous or juxtaposed ways. Clearly, in relational contexts where entities can take on any form, it is difficult to tell whether an animal is in human form, or a human in animal form. Key animal species in contemporary circumpolar societies can change scale and shape, so that a pine marten and an elk could potentially be the same being (see Ingold 1986: 251). If such ambiguities were part of Ertebølle society, then this may explain the location of the human body within an animal world, and the occasional transformation of the dead into corporate entities consisting of human and animal body parts. Ertebølle hunters seemingly did not reassemble the skeletons of their kills, but producing composite bodies and burying or burning some of them may have effected a similar act of renewal and repayment to those described in circumpolar ethnographies. Deposition of antler tines and pine marten carcasses at the water's edge at Ringkloster could be viewed as votive in this regard (see Bradley 2000: ch. 1). Future investigations of butchery techniques and the sharing of meat, as well as the structured deposition of remains, might be particularly fruitful in thinking about human social relations alongside spiritual engagement with animals. Finally, different animal species also practise distinct forms of sociality. Deer generally herd, with stags and does living in separate groups until late summer when social ties fracture into the mating season and stags try to acquire harems of does. Brown bears are solitary, while white-tailed eagles form breeding pairs. Animal species may therefore also have been emblematic of social relations between people, and different points in the social cycle may have been comparable to the aggregation of herds, flocks or schools of fish, for instance (cf. Tilley

1996: 65). The embedded nature of human existence in the animal world meant that social activity might have been understood through reference to animal sociality.

Articulating identities and relational personhood

If dividual features of the person were recognized, and body parts contained an element of personal soul, then the treatment of animal and human bodies was clearly an important spiritual matter. During earlier periods of the southern Scandinavian Mesolithic representations of human and animal bodies abound – there are very few convincing examples from the Ertebølle. Instead real bodies and their parts were used in social discourse, a trend that came to dominate Neolithic activity across northern Europe. The *presentation* of parts and wholes of real things were matters of concern, not their representation. Each person was a collection of elements from the whole cosmos, a fractal person that was also dividual to no slight degree. This dividuality could be altered through a version of partible relations during exchanges (cf. Strassburg 2000: 96–7); the sharing of food, during interactions with prey, and during mortuary practice where the person was extracted from one collective and given over to another. Some aspects of the dead were circulated among the human community, other parts might join the animal and spiritual community, and another aspect of their spirit might journey to another world. We could suggest, then, that monitoring bodily boundaries was actually of great importance, since each part of the body contained a spiritual element. If personhood was partible then compensating for loss of parts, for the leaching away of 'body-soul', was a social concern that social groups pursued in different ways, including, perhaps, through retention of some animal body parts.

Transformations between one state of personhood and another may have been enacted repeatedly throughout life – in rites of passage and communal dances, for example. One metaphor in this metamorphosis might be the removal of skin, and the human clothing in animal skin. Shifting skins might have marked shifting identities. The provision of some of the dead with antlers may have similar significance, conferring the ability to mimic deer in dialogic encounters (see Conneller 2001; Conneller and Yarrow 2002). Mimesis and dialogic action also suggests that patterns of action and comportment might have involved contextually specific identities, since each action might be a distinctive way of engaging with certain entities. Weaving a basket might therefore have engendered quite a different state of being to hunting a deer or trapping a pine marten. While we may trace one biographical individual through a string of acts, we could also consider a fully contextual and relational Ertebølle personhood dependent on current activity. Specific practices might have possessed people in different ways, allowing different aspects of their person to emerge. Durable individual identity might have been tempered against shifting and temporary interrelationships in which identities were presented contextually rather than accumulatively.

Personhood and social strategies: gender and age

Differentiation between men and women *within* specific age grades has been noted at Vedbaek (Strassburg 2000; Tilley 1996: 40-1), although overall gender distinctions between male and female bodies across southern Scandinavia were not standardized (Schmidt in press). Human and animal bodies may have been gendered performatively or substantially, and most likely through a mixture of both. Antlers regrow seasonally, forming a renewable source of substance. A stag with antlers might be quite a different entity to one without, and each substance (antler, teeth, fur/hair, blood, etc.) might have been 'charged' in specific ways. The body was arguably gendered in a multiple way, so that body parts and substances – both human and animal, both internal and attached to the body – were each gendered through their specific connotations and histories. The fixity or ambiguity of these substance-codes is open to question, but it would be misleading to gender only *entire* bodies male and female, just as it is misleading to assume any enduring fixity to bodily gender throughout life (Schmidt 2000; Hollimon 2000; Prine 2000). Acquisition of these materials through exchange practices perhaps demonstrated the efficacy of the person through their ability to elicit parts from human and non-human exchange partners, perhaps including entities like animal masters. We could imagine parallel gendered systems of exchange for furs, beads and antler-axes for instance (Weiner 1992; Strathern 1988), and/or a system of connections where such objects passed across genders in their exchange cycle. Teeth may have gendered parts of the person as male or female, or may have been shown up in a male or female way by association with particular activities. People pursued different strategies of transaction, and a certain amount of variability in those strategies may be observed in the diversity of mortuary practices and guises of the dead. One key issue in assessing gendering is that Eurasian shamans often encapsulate both male and female roles, substances and costumes (Zvelebil 1997; Schmidt 2000). If some or all of the corpses were those of ritual specialists this would greatly complicate the interpretation of two or more distinct genders.

These strategies seem to have had as much to do with age as gender. The elderly are almost devoid of manufactured goods, perhaps indicating that personhood changed throughout life so that the elderly became less multi-natural, plurally gendered beings and more like the anonymous herd animals that people would hunt. Conversely, some children received numerous grave goods, including flint tools they could not use. It is possible that as people passed through certain age grades so sets of materials were added to and removed from their bodies, and this was re-enacted through mortuary practices (see Alvi 2001). The elderly were perhaps at a stage in their lives characterized by giving and not receiving. They were identified with the herd, the regenerated antlers of the older stags – pure substance without task-specific form. This might also have denoted a particular gender for this age group – a 'post-reproductive' gender, for instance, who could cope with raw fertile substance. Whatever strategies for dealing in the essences of the world people pursued throughout life in transforming and maintaining personhood, these were mutually-authored. Just as people of certain age-grades may give or receive in different ways, so others will give to and receive from them accordingly. The treatment of the dead is no different, and so may afford information about certain facets of the perceived relational identities of the dead.

Death

As argued in previous chapters, changing the appearance of the body can change the nature of being. Relationships between kinds in the aceramic Ertebølle might have employed something like a multi-natural logic, in which bodies could be moved across social boundaries. Perhaps Ertebølle communities saw all persons, whether primarily human or animal, as able to shift their forms through interaction with one another. Ertebølle people had mutable bodies, and we could suggest that one aspect of a human became animal after death. While objects are key to interactions, the elder members of the community were perhaps so adept at taking on a series of different perspectives that their bodies required minimal material assistance for transformation. For others, jaws, teeth and other body parts each mediated flows of essences in different ways. Placing fish in graves might facilitate movement through the underworld, birds the upper world. The offering of the dead may itself have been vital in renewing relationships, and, in the case of the elderly, transferring qualities of key members of the community from the human kin to deer herds, from hunters to prey. Perhaps the animal world was the destination of one element of the person, while another departed to a different community. If we accept a tripartite model of the cosmos as an appropriate analogy, then cremation would deliver some spiritual component into the heavens, while burial in land or under water would either retain essences in the world of the living or send them into the underworld. Mortuary practices might address community concerns about where such essences should be directed (cf. Strassburg 229–34). This may in part be based on the individual biographies of the deceased, but features of that biography such as whether or not they died suddenly may have little to do with their individuality. The dead played a very specific role in mediating between the living and the ancestral dead, one world and another, humans and other animals. Further to this, all people interacted with animals throughout their lives, and it is possible that animal trophies were taken to keep a part of the animal within the person, or even recover a part of the person extracted in the relational encounter. Shamans might donate animal body parts to the deceased, returning lost parts of the person in the unifying act before the person was finally dispersed. Mortuary practice possibly 'completed' the person, providing the basis for dissolution into other orders of being, perhaps including continued personhood in a different form. Certain codes would apply to how personhood should be achieved and maintained, though strategies for engaging with that logic were variable. Sacrificial death for humans in the Ertebølle also cannot be ruled out, if only in a similar sense to the Hindu conception of a sacrificial death. Lastly, if burials took place at a time of communal gathering and were accompanied by feasts, then a system of mortuary exchanges can be inferred. The dissolution of the person into component parts, some of which were material like beads and perhaps acquired a distinct personhood of their own, was therefore incorporated within acts of integration and social renewal.

Attitude

Clearly wild animals were preyed upon; they were hunted and trapped. This does not in itself indicate a predatory relationship. These hunting practices can, however, be contextualized alongside the killing and injuring of a fairly high proportion of humans buried at Ertebølle sites. The kind of treatment we can see extended to humans, animals and objects is both violent and reciprocal. Although these communities hunted animals they did not do so in a way that was excessively exploitative or predatory. While animals were killed and eaten, humans were killed too, and may also have been eaten by animals (which were in turn a kind of person) and possibly spirits. Human deaths were in some cases accompanied by the reciprocal death of an animal (e.g. the decapitated dog with the woman in grave XIII, Skateholm II). But something seemed to demand the death of certain human beings too. The violence behind this kind of reciprocity may be similar to the kind of violence Descola (1996: 90) identifies with predatory exchanges in parts of South America. Exchanges are rarely benign, and carry debts and obligations – in some cases those exchanges between the human and the non-human world may have taken the form of violent sacrifices. Furthermore, the system of exchanges which took place may seem to be reciprocal and far-reaching, but modes of relations in gift-giving can also be aggressive. Gift-giving can mediate conflict without recourse to open violence, but violent extraction of essences from people and animals may also have been an important goal in itself. It is possible to imagine a mixture of reciprocal and predatory relations, therefore. Human life alongside dogs could also be described as mutual protection. Domesticated animals, dogs, were not preyed upon, and were treated with the same care after death as human beings – even when that 'care' was violent.

Conclusion

This chapter illustrates how a focus on features of personhood aside from individuality complements or even offers an alternative to such an approach. I have suggested an interpretation that illustrates how we can imagine past people from a relational point of view, in a way that does not present them as dupes of cultural determinism or as bounded and self-expressive individualists. I have argued that the people buried in the Ertebølle cemeteries consisted of multiple elements, the incorporation and/or practical use of which actively transformed their natures. 'Grave goods' were not simple markers of social status, but central to the mediation of relations between a host of social beings. Human communities can identify objects, plants, animals and even places as persons or quasi-persons, or supernatural and superhuman beings. We cannot assume them to be objects or 'dumb' animals rather than persons of one kind or another, and can consider contexts through which that personhood emerges, is transformed and even sublimated. An attempt to define personhood in the past cannot simply focus on the human body and ignore the treatment of these other kinds of body, which may also be persons and parts of persons. While the interpretation forwarded here is only one possibility, and drawing on different analogies might alter it dramatically, it does illustrate the rewards that can be gained from studying trends in the practices through which prehistoric personhood was experienced, cited, interpreted and actively manipulated.

CONCLUSION

Relational personhood in context

Introduction

The archaeology of personhood operates through the study of personal transactions, relationships, interactions and transformations. Personhood gives a shape to how identities that shift continually throughout life are mediated through the small interactions between a few people, and in large community events, through sharing, cooking and eating food, through death and decomposition and through mortuary exchanges and ancestral ceremonies. It is not just individuals who can be persons, and personhood is not just a matter of individuality. Sometimes an entity is perceived as a person, sometimes not; sometimes individual biography might be brought to the fore, while at other times the person is thrown into relief as highly dividual, and even as a 'stereotypical' social figure playing a role. I have argued that personhood is richly cultural, and yet the attainment of personhood arises from political conditions and social strategies. While trends in personhood therefore provide the format for social interaction, the attainment of personhood itself involves the incorporation of other features of identity like gender, sex, sexuality, ethnicity, caste, religion and divinity. However, 'identity' is a very broad term with a range of applications. Although it can also be used in a variety of ways, 'personhood' is a specific term for the condition of being a person as conceptualized by a given community. This condition is understood and formulated through modes of personhood

155

which provide the conceptual and practical frames that also structure the possibilities for gendering, caste and so on. Yet even something as basic as personhood may be mutable and contextual, may be now apparent in one way and then transformed or even absent throughout the biography of a human being, community, animal or artefact. Since personhood is heavily entangled with other factors of identity, there can be no single definition that applies to all contexts, nor any single process through which personhood is attained. For these reasons I have not advocated a separate archaeology of personhood, but rather suggested that the trends through which personhood is produced form a central piece in the puzzle of our theoretical struggle with past identities. Principles in practice like partibility and the transmission of substances are therefore vital features in understanding not only personhood but identities in general. The studies reviewed in this book all illustrate the significance of personhood alongside other features of identity, and open up avenues for interpreting even the most fragmented of remains in fruitful and exciting ways.

From ethnographic basis to archaeological framework

While the precise mechanics of Melanesian partibility and its attendant understanding of the world may be specific to Melanesia, the idea that there were different prehistoric trends involving partibility does not seem far-fetched. It is certainly as likely as prehistoric people conceiving of themselves as indivisible individuals. Given the strength of evidence for fragmented and distributed bodies in the past, and for interpersonal exchanges in a non-capitalist world, I consider it far more likely. That persons risk losing parts of themselves in relations with animals in northern Eurasian cosmology is just one example of how widespread relational and dividual features of personhood are. Dividuality is clearly a feature of personhood we can expect in past contexts. While rendering ethnographic studies of personhood in a simplified but hopefully still faithful form, I have also reconfigured the concepts of mediated and unmediated exchange, and permeability and partibility, for archaeological purposes. I have suggested that the flow of substances through permeable people could be imagined alongside partible relations in past contexts. This would seem to undermine the differences apparent in the two ethnographic constructs, since the flow of substances in Melanesia is a factor of partibility. However, from an archaeological point of view it is important to recognize both the differences apparent in these structuring principles and the potential for cultural change, and overlaps between seemingly divergent trends. We need not reify past people as partible or permeable any more than they have already been reified as individuals: they were simply people. Rather, we can focus on social practices like partibility as a more extreme version of the permeability of the body, and then discuss the strategies that people pursued in operating relationships that stressed the partiblity, permeability or indivisibility of the person in different ways. However, while it has been argued here that trends in permeable and partible personhood existed alongside individuality in the past, it should be remembered that all of these concepts derive from very specific interpretations of modern societies. Archaeologists are able to use these ethnographic constructs analytically, but we cannot ignore the way they colour our view of the past. While individuality alone is myopic, and further lenses must be ground to refocus the eye, we have perhaps only seen the beginning of this process in archaeology over the last ten years.

I have suggested more generally that past people negotiated individuality and dividuality in a range of different ways. The basic approach taken (in broad agreement with LiPuma 1998 and Chapman 2000) is that there are two *imagined* extreme positions of Western individuality and extremely relational personhood, but that all societies provide frameworks for people to negotiate features of both. I have suggested a range of heuristics including a broad tension between relational, dividual and fractal personhood associated with inalienable relations at one end of a spectrum, and fixed, individual personhood with representational metaphors and alienable relations at the other. Distinct cultural fields of possibility, which I have glossed as modes of personhood, frame negotiations between these, often tipping the balance heavily in favour of one end of the spectrum. Inalienability, dividuality and fractal personhood are parallel ways of describing the same phenomenon on a very broad level (see Chapman 2000: 29–32, 48), but there are also a range of different strategies and logics of personhood that fall within the bounds of these terms. The implications of this approach extend beyond how we think about people, to how we understand the rest of the world. The principles structuring personhood discussed here as analogies for past personhood provide an alternative to imagining past people as individuated from the world and conducting relations with fully externalized others.

Personhood, agency and individuals

It should be clear that sidelining the individual is not an attempt to dehumanize the past but to better illustrate how human beings may be situated in the world and recognize that human experience internalizes features of that world in a highly significant way. Attending repeatedly to the structure and form of personhood may seem overly deterministic. I have largely focused on the conditions for personhood, and trends in how personhood is realized. These cultural conditions enable different kinds of interactions, and some foster individuality in a way that others do not. But people themselves mutually negotiate events, and ultimately interpret and revise personhood itself. People are not themselves reflections of a mode of personhood: a mode of personhood provides the frame of reference within which people engage with one another. Modes of personhood are reflected upon, sometimes critically, as are the social trends that support them. One critique of this book may be that it does not really get to grips with the lives of any specific individuals: past ones in terms of the archaeology, and present ones in terms of the anthropology. This is not my goal, but that does not mean that such accounts are without value. Personhood beyond individuality is not personhood without individuals. We can consider the individual person as one presentation among many, one state among others, one aspect of every person. We need not do away with individuals in the past, though I suggest that we need not feel obliged to place great emphasis on individuating past people when other aspects of their personhood remain unstudied. If we are interested in individual lives and experiences, then full use can be made of studies of individual, permeable, dividual and partible lives at the same time.

The tension between individuality and community is not always the most relevant tension in a fractal world where the community is internalized in each person, and each person may contain a part of another. It presumes an inside and outside to the person in a way not so relevant in more relational personhood where the person is also immersed in places and practices (e.g. Ingold 2000d). In many cases this tension has occupied far too prominent a place in archaeology. In its place we could consider how trends in personhood provided a realm of possibilities and motivations for individuals and collectives, and also non-human beings, however they interpenetrated one another. Kinship groups, age sets, gender groups such as men's cults, caste groups: these differing axes along which societies may be organized are of varying importance in each social context. They may therefore be core to the generative relations through which personhood is attained and maintained, and the motivations of each subcommunity and person. People act with a conception of personhood in mind. They act within the framework of existing trends in relationships. Their actions produce personhood, but all actions are interactive so they do not form their own personhood alone.

Ambiguity, personhood, community and cosmos

Archaeological investigation of personhood relies on interpreting the media and remains of past actions, and strategies in the repeated redeployment of those media. A methodological approach to parts and wholes is an important feature of such an approach, but so is the acknowledgement that conceptions of what constitutes a part and a whole are themselves contextual. While material culture is used in citing relations of personhood it is in no way a reflection of a social reality. We will not know for certain whether or when anthropomorphic pots, or swords, or round houses were thought of as people, and by whom, or how contested such identities might have been. The elasticity of our own concept of personhood is rather limited. This may also have been so in the past, though the basic shape of the concept was often probably quite different to our own. I have forwarded the view that it does not matter whether past things were definitively people or not: what matters is the effect that they have on social relations. Furthermore, personhood of one kind or another may emerge in certain situations but not others. Personhood is not a quality that necessarily automatically belongs to or does not belong to any entity. Orokaiva pigs can be persons, but during childhood initiation rites they are separated out as a distinct category that can be eaten through the rest of life: yet this distinction between humans and pigs is undone upon death (Barraud *et al.* 1994: 36–7). The statuses of humans and animals are, through transformations in personhood, interlinked here, and those distinctions revised throughout life as personhood takes on new dimensions for those concerned. In a highly relational world, such as that described as animistic, personhood may be so temporary and conditional that any fixed notion of what is and is not a person based on the form of the thing would be almost meaningless. It is what things and animals and non-human entities *do* that allows them to be understood as persons. Ultimately, then, personhood can only be understood through interpretation of the transactions between people, and between people and things, substances, buildings, animals and other entities. Some modes of personhood immerse people in the world so that their substance is its substance, their community is the community of the cosmos. The dissolution of bodies and redistribution of body parts may be vital to the circulation of energy among all living things. It has been impossible, then, to write a book on personhood in the past without discussing death and the regeneration of life and the circulation of substances throughout the cosmos. Taken to its full extent a relational and fractal world actually requires us to see all phenomena as either persons, potentially persons, or constitutive of persons, and to immerse human beings in a 'total field of relations'

(Ingold 2000d: 108). This way of thinking will obviously be relevant to some contexts and alien to others. It certainly has uses for our interpretation of European prehistory.

Personhood and the archaeological imagination

Archaeologists are concerned with the human past. Humanizing the past does not simply mean 'add individuals and stir'. In interpreting personhood it is necessary to present a humanized view of the past, but it is also important to people the past with different human and non-human beings, with personified places, objects, communities, ancestors and spirits. Archaeologists are increasingly willing to accord material phenomena the status of our partners in agency: it should not be unreasonable to think that past human beings also thought of them as partners in a social world. Archaeologists have much to offer other social sciences in ongoing attempts to understand the full range of personhood through patterns in past practices, past material worlds. This may perhaps only be achieved if archaeologists attempt to move across many contexts – present as well as past – and take on the burden of the difficult mediation between the universal and the specific, the particular and the general, the brief and the long term. In the end there is seemingly no limit to what a person might be and what might be a person. The archaeological imagination is well stocked to explore the range of possibilities for personhood in the past, and this book has illustrated how explicit analytical frameworks for this exploration are taking shape.

REFERENCES

Albrethsen, S. and Brinch Petersen, E. (1976) 'Excavation of a Mesolithic cemetery at Vedbaek, Denmark', *Acta Archaeologica* 47: 1–28.

Alvi, A. (2001) 'The category of the person in rural Punjab', *Social Anthropology* 9 (1): 45–63.

Andersen, S. (1991) 'Bjørnsholm. A stratified køkkenmodding on the Central Limford, North Jutland', *Journal of Danish Archaeology* 10: 58–96.

—— (1995) 'Ringkloster: Ertebølle trappers and wild boar hunters in eastern Jutland', *Journal of Danish Archaeology* 12: 13–59.

Appadurai, A. (1986) 'Introduction: commodities and the politics of value', in A. Appadurai (ed.) *The Social Life of Things: Commodities in Cultural Perspective*, 3–63. Cambridge: Cambridge University Press.

Barley, N. (1995) *Dancing on the Grave: Encounters with Death*. London: John Murray.

Barraud, C., de Coppet, D., Iteanu, A. and Jamous, R. (1994) *Of Relations and the Dead: Four Societies Viewed from the Angle of their Exchanges*. Oxford: Berg.

Barrett, J. (1988a) 'Fields of discourse: reconstituting a social archaeology', *Critique of Anthropology* 7 (3): 5–16.

—— (1988b) 'The living, the dead and the ancestors: Neolithic and early Bronze Age mortuary practices', in J. Barrett and I. Kinnes (eds) *The Archaeology of Context in the Neolithic and Bronze Age*, 30–41. Sheffield: Department of Prehistory and Archaeology.

—— (1994) *Fragments from Antiquity: An Archaeology of Social Life in Britain, 2900–1200 BC*. Oxford: Blackwell.

—— (2000) 'A thesis on agency', in M.-A. Dobres and J.E. Robb (eds) *Agency in Archaeology*, 61–8. London: Routledge.

—— (2001) 'Agency, the duality of structure, and the problem of the archaeological record', in I. Hodder (ed.) *Archaeological Theory Today*, 141–64. Cambridge: Polity Press.

Battaglia, D. (1990) *On the Bones of the Serpent: Person, Memory and Mortality in Sabarl Society.* Chicago: Chicago University Press.

—— (1991) 'Punishing the yams: leadership and gender ambivalence on Sabarl Island', in M. Godelier and M. Strathern (eds) *Big Men and Great Men*, 83–96. Cambridge: Cambridge University Press.

—— (1995) 'Problematizing the self: a thematic introduction', in D. Battaglia (ed.) *Rhetorics of Self-making*, 1–15. Berkeley: University of California Press.

Bazelmans, J. (2002) 'Moralities of dress and the dress of the dead in early medieval Europe', in Y. Hamilakis, M. Pluciennik and S. Tarlow (eds) *Thinking Through the Body: Archaeologies of Corporeality*, 71–84. London: Kluwer/Academic Press.

Becker, A. (1995) *Body, Self and Society: The View from Fiji.* Philadelphia: University of Pennsylvania Press.

Bird-David, N. (1993) 'Tribal metaphorization of human–nature relatedness – a comparative analysis', in K. Milton (ed.) *Environmentalism: The View from Anthropology*, 112–25. London: Routledge.

—— (1999) '"Animism" revisited: personhood, environment, and relational epistemology', *Current Anthropology* 40: 67–92.

Bloch, M. (1971) *Placing the Dead.* London: Seminar Press.

—— (1982) 'Death, women and power', in M. Bloch and J. Parry (eds) *Death and the Regeneration of Life*, 211–30. Cambridge: Cambridge University Press.

—— (1989) 'Death and the concept of the person', in S. Cederroth, C. Corlin and J. Lindstrom (eds) *On the Meaning of Death*, 11–29. Cambridge: Cambridge University Press.

—— (1995) 'Questions not to ask of Malagasy carvings', in I. Hodder, M. Shanks, A. Alexandri, V. Buchli, J. Carman, J. Last and G. Lucas (eds) *Interpreting Archaeology*, 212–15. London: Routledge.

Bloch, M. and Parry, J. (1982) 'Introduction: death and the regeneration of life', in M. Bloch and J. Parry (eds) *Death and the Regeneration of Life*, 1–44. Cambridge: Cambridge University Press.

Bordo, S. (1987) *The Flight to Objectivity: Essays on Cartesianism and Culture.* Albany: State University of New York Press.

Bourdieu, P. (1977) *Outline of a Theory of Practice.* Cambridge: Cambridge University Press.

—— (1990) *The Logic of Practice* (trans. R. Nice). Cambridge: Polity Press.

Boyd, B. (2002) 'Ways of eating, ways of being in the later Epipalaeolithic (Natufian) Levant', in Y. Hamilakis, M. Pluciennik and S. Tarlow (eds) *Thinking Through the Body: Archaeologies of Corporeality*, 137–52. London: Kluwer/Academic Press.

Bradley, R. (1998) *The Significance of Monuments.* London: Routledge.

—— (2000) *The Archaeology of Natural Places.* London: Routledge.

—— (2002) *The Past in Prehistoric Societies.* London: Routledge.

Braidotti, R. (1991) *Patterns of Dissonance.* Cambridge: Polity Press.

Brinch Petersen, E. and MeikleJohn, C. (2003) 'Three cremations and a funeral: aspects of burial practice in Mesolithic Vedbaek', in L. Larsson, H. Kindgren, K. Knutsson, D. Leoffler and A. Åkerlund (eds) *Mesolithic on the Move*, 485–93. Oxford: Oxbow Books.

Brück, J. (1995) 'A place for the dead: the role of human remains in the Late Bronze Age', *Proceedings of the Prehistoric Society* 61: 245–77.

—— (1999) 'Houses, lifecycles and deposition on Middle Bronze Age settlements in southern England', *Proceedings of the Prehistoric Society* 65: 145–66.

—— (2001a) 'Body metaphors and technologies of transformation in the English Middle and Late Bronze Age', in J. Brück (ed.) *Bronze Age Landscapes: Tradition and Transformation*, 149–60. Oxford: Oxbow.

—— (2001b) 'Monuments, power and personhood in the British Neolithic', *Journal of the Royal Anthropological Institute* 7: 649–67.

Burrow, S. (1997) *The Neolithic Culture of the Isle of Man.* Oxford: British Archaeological Reports British Series 263.

Busby, C. (1997) 'Permeable and partible persons: a comparative analysis of gender and the body in South India and Melanesia', *Journal of the Royal Anthropological Institute* 3 (2): 261–78.

—— (1999) 'Agency, power and personhood: discourses of gender and violence in a fishing community in south India', *Critique of Anthropology* 19 (3): 227–48.

Butler, J. (1990) *Gender Trouble: Feminism and the Subversion of Identity.* New York: Routledge.

—— (1993) *Bodies that Matter: on the Discursive Limits of 'Sex'.* New York: Routledge.

—— (1994) 'Bodies that matter', in C. Burke, N. Schor and M. Whitford (eds) *Engaging with Irigaray: Feminist Philosophy and Modern European Thought*, 142–67. New York: Columbia University Press.

Carrithers, M., Collins, S. and Lukes, S. (eds) (1985) *The Category of the Person: Anthropology, Philosophy, History.* Cambridge: Cambridge University Press.

REFERENCES

Chapman, J. (1996) 'Enchainment, commodification, and gender in the Balkan Copper Age', *Journal of European Archaeology* 4: 203–42.

—— (2000) *Fragmentation in Archaeology: People, Places and Broken Objects in the Prehistory of South-Eastern Europe.* London: Routledge.

—— (2002a) 'Partible people and androgynous figurines in the Balkan Neolithic', Paper presented at University of Manchester TAG 2002, session entitled 'Personhood and the Material World'.

—— (2002b) 'Colourful prehistories: the problem with the Berlin and Kay colour paradigm', in A. Jones and G. MacGregor (eds) *Colouring the Past*, 45–72. Oxford: Berg.

Clarke, D.V., Cowie, T. and Foxon, A. (1985) *Symbols of Power at the Time of Stonehenge.* Edinburgh: HMSO.

Cohen, A. (1994) *Self Consciousness: An Alternative Anthropology of Identity.* London: Routledge.

Conneller, C. (2001) 'Becoming deer: corporeal transformations at Star Carr', Paper presented at University College Dublin TAG 2001, session entitled 'Construction Sites'.

Conneller, C. and Yarrow, T. (2002) 'Assembling animals', Paper presented at University of Manchester TAG 2002, session entitled 'Personhood and the Material World'.

Connerton, P. (1990) *How Societies Remember.* Cambridge: Cambridge University Press.

Csordas, T. (1999) 'Embodiment and cultural phenomenology', in G. Weiss and H. Faber (eds) *Perspectives on Embodiment: The Intersections of Nature and Culture*, 143–62. London: Routledge.

Cummings, V. (2002) 'Experiencing texture and touch in the British Neolithic', *Oxford Journal of Archaeology* 21: 249–61.

Darvill, T. (2001) 'Neolithic enclosures in the Isle of Man', in T. Darvill and J. Thomas (eds) *Neolithic Enclosures in North-west Europe*, 77–111. Oxford: Oxbow.

—— (2002) 'White on blond: quartz pebbles and the use of quartz at Neolithic monuments in the Isle of Man and beyond', in A. Jones and G. MacGregor (eds) *Colouring the Past*, 73–92. Oxford: Berg.

Darwin, C. (1859) *On the Origin of Species.* London: John Murray.

Davey, P. and Woodcock, J. (in press) 'Rheast Buigh, Patrick: middle Neolithic exploitation of the Manx uplands?', in I. Armit, E. Murphy, E. Nelis and D. Simpson (eds) *Neolithic Settlement in Ireland and Western Britain.* Oxford: Oxbow Books.

Dawkins, R. (1976) *The Selfish Gene.* Oxford: Oxford University Press.

REFERENCES

De Coppet, D. (1981) 'The life-giving death', in S. Humphreys and H. King (eds) *Mortality and Immortality: the Anthropology and Archaeology of Death*, 175–204. London: Academic Press.

Deetz, J. (1977) *In Small Things Forgotten: The Archaeology of Early American Life*. New York: Anchor.

Dennett, D. (1995) *Darwin's Dangerous Idea*. Harmondsworth: Penguin Books.

Derrida, J. (1986). 'Différance', in M. Taylor (ed.) *Deconstruction in Context: Literature and Philosophy*. Chicago, Ill.: University of Chicago Press.

Descola, P. (1996) 'Constructing natures: symbolic ecology and social practice', in P. Descola and G. Palsson (eds) *Nature and Society: Anthropological Perspectives*, 82–102. London: Routledge.

Devisch, R. (1993) *Weaving the Threads of Life: The Khita Gyn-eco-logical Healing Cult among the Yaka*. Chicago, Ill.: University of Chicago Press.

Dobres, M.-A. (1999) *Technology and Social Agency*. Oxford: Batsford.

Douglas, M. and Ney, S. (1998) *Missing Persons: A Critique of Personhood in the Social Sciences*. Berkeley: University of California Press.

Edmonds, M. (1997) 'Taskscape, technology and tradition', *Analecta Praehistorica Leidensia* 29: 99–110.

Eriksson, G. and Zagorska, I. (2003) 'Do dogs eat like humans? Marine stable isotope signals in dog teeth from inland Zvejnieki', in L. Larsson, H. Kindgren, K. Knutsson, D. Leoffler and A. Åkerlund (eds) *Mesolithic on the Move*, 160–8. Oxford: Oxbow Books.

Featherstone, M. (ed.) (2000) *Body Modification*. London: Sage.

Finlay, N. (2003) 'Microliths and multiple authorship', in L. Larsson, H. Kindgren, K. Knutsson, D. Leoffler and A. Åkerlund (eds) *Mesolithic on the Move*, 169–76. Oxford: Oxbow Books.

Fortes, M. (1987) *Religion, Morality and the Person: Essays on Tallensi Religion* (edited by J. Goody). Cambridge: Cambridge University Press.

Foucault, M. (1977) *Discipline and Punish*. Harmondsworth: Penguin.

—— (1984) On the genealogy of ethics: an overview of work in progress, in P. Rabinow (ed.) *The Foucault Reader*, 340–72. New York: Pantheon Books.

Fowler, C. (1997) 'Experiencing the future: flashback, vivid memory and the materialisation of temporality in Melanesian societies', *Diatribe* 7: 69–82.

—— (2000) 'The subject, the individual, and archaeological interpretation: reading Judith Butler and Luce Irigaray', in C. Holtorf and H. Karlsson (eds) *Philosophy and Archaeological Practice: Perspectives for the 21st Century*, 107–35. Gothenburg: Bricoleur Press.

—— (2001) 'Personhood and social relations in the British Neolithic, with a study from the Isle of Man', *Journal of Material Culture* 6 (2): 137–63.

—— (2002) 'Body parts: Personhood and materiality in the Manx Neolithic', in Y. Hamilakis, M. Pluciennik and S. Tarlow (eds) *Thinking Through the Body: Archaeologies of Corporeality*, 47–69. London: Kluwer/ Academic Press.

—— (2003) 'Rates of (ex)change: decay and growth, memory and the transformation of the dead in early Neolithic southern Britain', in H. Williams (ed.) *Archaeologies of Remembrance – Death and Memory in Past Societies*, 45–63. New York: Kluwer Academic/ Plenum Press.

—— (in press) 'In touch with the past? Bodies, monuments and the sacred in the Manx Neolithic', in V. Cummings and C. Fowler (eds) *The Neolithic of the Irish Sea: Materiality and Traditions of Practice*, Oxford: Oxbow Books.

Fowler, C. and Cummings, V. (2003) 'Places of transformation: building monuments from water and stone in the Neolithic of the Irish Sea', *Journal of the Royal Anthropological Institute* 9: 1–20.

Gatens, M. (1992) 'Power, bodies and difference', in M. Barrett and A. Phillips (eds) *Destabilizing Theory: Contemporary Feminist Debates*, 120–37. Cambridge: Polity Press.

Gell, A. (1993) *Wrapping in Images: Tattooing in Polynesia*. Oxford: Clarendon.

—— (1998) *Art and Agency: An Anthropological Theory*. Oxford: Clarendon.

—— (1999) 'Strathernograms, or the semiotics of mixed metaphors', in E. Hirsch (ed.) *The Art of Anthropology: Essays and Diagrams: Alfred Gell*, 29–75. London: Athlone.

Gero, J. and Conkey, M. (eds) (1991) *Engendering Archaeology: Women and Prehistory*. Oxford: Blackwell.

Ghosh, S. (1989) *Hindu Concept of Life and Death*. New Delhi: Munshiram Manoharlal.

Giambelli, R. (1998) 'The coconut, the body and the human being: metaphors of life and growth in Nusa Penida and Bali', in L. Rival (ed.) *The Social Life of Trees: Anthropological Perspectives on Tree Symbolism*. Oxford: Berg.

Giddens, A. (1990) *The Consequences of Modernity*. Cambridge: Polity Press.

—— (1991) *Modernity and Self-identity*. Cambridge: Polity Press.

Gilchrist, R. (1999) *Gender and Archaeology: Contesting the Past*. London: Routledge.

Glob, P. (1969) *The Bog People*. London: Faber and Faber.

Godelier, M. (1999) *The Enigma of the Gift* (trans. N. Scott). Chicago, Ill.: University of Chicago Press.

Godelier, M. and Strathern, M. (eds) (1991) *Big Men and Great Men: Personifications of Power in Melanesia.* Cambridge: Cambridge University Press.

Goodenough, W. (1969) 'Rethinking "status" and "role": Toward a general model of the cultural organization of social relationships', in S. Tyler (ed.) *Cognitive Anthropology*, 311–30. New York: Holt, Rinehart and Winston.

Gosden, C. (1994) *Social Being and Time.* Oxford: Blackwell.

—— (1999) *Anthropology and Archaeology: A Changing Relationship.* London: Routledge.

Grigson, C. (1989) 'Bird-foraging patterns in the Mesolithic', in C. Bonsall (ed.) *The Mesolithic in Europe*, 60–72. Edinburgh: John Donald.

Grøn, O. and Skaarup, J. (1991) 'Møllegabet II: a submerged Mesolithic site and a boat burial from Aerø', *Journal of Danish Archaeology* 10: 38–50.

Hamilakis, Y. (2002) 'The past as oral history: towards an archaeology of the senses', in Y. Hamilakis, M. Pluciennik and S. Tarlow (eds) *Thinking Through the Body: Archaeologies of Corporeality*, 121–36. London: Kluwer/ Academic Press.

Hamilakis, Y., Pluciennik, M. and Tarlow, S. (eds) (2002) *Thinking Through the Body: Archaeologies of Corporeality.* London: Kluwer/Academic Press.

Hebdige, D. (1979) *Subcultures: On the Meaning of Style.* London: Methuen.

Hekman, S.J. (1990) *Gender and Knowledge: Elements of a Postmodern Feminism*, Boston, Mass.: Northeastern University Press.

Helms, M. (1993) *Craft and the Kingly Ideal: Art, Trade and Power.* Austin: Texas University Press.

Hirsch, E. (1990) 'From bones to betelnuts: processes of ritual transformation and the development of "national culture" in Papua New Guinea', *Man* 25: 18–34.

Hodder, I. (1982) *The Present Past.* Oxford: Batsford.

—— (1986) *Reading the Past: Current Approaches to Interpretation in Archaeology.* Cambridge: Cambridge University Press.

—— (2000) 'Agency and individuals in long-term processes', in M.-A. Dobres and J. Robb (eds) *Agency in Archaeology*, 21–33. New York: Routledge.

Holck, P. (1987) *Cremated Bones: A Medical Anthropological Study of an Archaeological Material on Cremation Burials.* Oslo: University of Oslo.

Hollimon, S. (2000) 'Archaeology of the *'Aqi*: gender and sexuality in prehistoric Chumash society', in R. Schmidt and B. Voss (eds) *The Archaeology of Sexuality*, 179–96. London: Routledge.

Howell, S. (1989) 'Of persons and things: exchange and valuables among the Lio of eastern Indonesia', *Man* 24: 419–38.

—— (1996) 'Nature in culture or culture in nature? Chewong ideas of "humans" and other species', in P. Descola and G. Palsson (eds) *Nature and Society: Anthropological Perspectives*, 127–44. London: Routledge.

Ingold, T. (1986) *The Appropriation of Nature: Essays on Human Ecology and Social Relations*. Manchester: Manchester University Press.

—— (1988) 'Introduction', in T. Ingold (ed.) *What is an Animal?*, 1–16. London: Routledge.

—— (1993) 'The temporality of the landscape', *World Archaeology* 25: 152–74.

—— (1994) 'From trust to domination: an alternative history of human–animal relations', in A. Manning and J. Sperbell (eds) *Animals and Human Society: Changing Perspectives*, 1–22. London: Routledge.

—— (1996) 'Growing plants and raising animals: an anthropological perspective', in D. Harris (ed.) *The Origins and Spread of Farming in Eurasia*, 12–24. London: UCL Press.

—— (2000a) 'Making things, growing plants, raising animals and bringing up children', in T. Ingold, *The Perception of the Environment: Essays in Livelihood, Dwelling and Skill*, 77–88. London: Routledge.

—— (2000b) 'Totemism, animism and the depiction of animals', in T. Ingold, *The Perception of the Environment: Essays in Livelihood, Dwelling and Skill*, 111–31. London: Routledge.

—— (2000c) 'Ancestry, generation, substance, memory, land', in T. Ingold, *The Perception of the Environment: Essays in Livelihood, Dwelling and Skill*, 132–51. London: Routledge.

—— (2000d) 'A circumpolar night's dream', in T. Ingold, *The Perception of the Environment: Essays in Livelihood, Dwelling and Skill*, 89–110. London: Routledge.

—— (2000e) *The Perception of the Environment: Essays in Livelihood, Dwelling and Skill*. London: Routledge.

Irigaray, L. (1985) *This Sex Which Is Not One* (trans. C. Porter, with C. Burke). London: Athlone Press.

Iteanu, A. (1988) 'The concept of the person and the ritual system: an Orokaiva view', *Man* 25: 35–53.

—— (1995) 'Rituals and ancestors', in D. de Coppet and A. Iteanu (eds) *Cosmos and Society in Oceania*, 135–63. Oxford: Berg.

Jones, A. (1998) 'Where eagles dare: landscape, animals and the Neolithic of Orkney', *Journal of Material Culture* 3 (3): 301–24.

—— (2002a) 'A biography of colour: colour, material histories and personhood in the early Bronze Age of Britain and Ireland', in A. Jones and G. MacGregor (eds) *Colouring the Past*, 159–74. Oxford: Berg.

—— (2002b) *Archaeological Theory and Scientific Practice.* Cambridge: Cambridge University Press.

Jones, A. and Richards, C. (2003) 'Animals into ancestors: domestication, food and identity in late Neolithic Orkney', in M. Parker Pearson (ed.) *Food, Culture and Identity in the Neolithic and Early Bronze Age*, 45–51. Oxford: BAR International Series 1117.

Jones, S. (1997) *The Archaeology of Ethnicity.* London: Routledge.

Jonsson, L. (1986) 'Fish bones in late Mesolithic human graves at Skateholm, southern Sweden', in D. Brinkhuizen and A. Clason (eds) *Fish and Archaeology: Studies in Osteometry, Taphonomy, Seasonality and Fishing Methods*, 62–79. Oxford: BAR International Series 294.

Jordanova, L. (1989) *Sexual Visions: Images of Gender in Science and Medicine between the Eighteenth and Twentieth Centuries.* London: Harvester-Wheatsheaf.

Joyce, R. (2000) *Gender and Power in Prehispanic Mesoamerica.* Austin: University of Texas Press.

Keates, S. (2002) 'The flashing blade: copper, colour and luminosity in north Italian Copper Age society', in A. Jones and G. MacGregor (eds) *Colouring the Past*, 109–27. Oxford: Berg.

Kent, S. (1989) 'Cross-cultural perceptions of farmers as hunters and the value of meat', in S. Kent (ed.) *Farmers as Hunters*, 1–17. Cambridge: Cambridge University Press.

Kirtsoglou, E. (2002) 'Objects of affection: material tales of the Greek periphery', Paper presented at University of Manchester TAG 2002, session entitled 'The Uses and Abuses of Ethnography'.

Knapp, A. and Meskell, L. (1997) 'Bodies of evidence on prehistoric Cyprus', *Cambridge Archaeological Journal* 7 (2): 183–204.

Knutsson, H. (2000) 'Two technologies: two mentalities', in H. Knutsson (ed.) *Halvvägs kust till kust: stenålderssamhällen I förändring*, 11–41. Gothenburg: Department of Archaeology.

Kopytoff, I. (1986) 'The cultural biography of things: commoditization as process', in A. Appadurai (ed.) *The Social Life of Things: Commodities in Cultural Perspective*, 64–91. Cambridge: Cambridge University Press.

Lakoff, G. and Johnson, N. (1980) *Metaphors We Live By.* Chicago, Ill.: University of Chicago Press.

Larsson, L. (1983) *Ageröd V*. Lund: Acta Archaeologica Lundensia.

—— (1988) (ed.) *The Skateholm Project I: Man and Environment*. Stockholm: Almqvist and Wiksell.

—— (1989a) 'Big dog and poor man. Mortuary practices in Mesolithic societies in southern Sweden', in T. Larsson and H. Lundmark (eds) *Approaches to Swedish Archaeology*, 211–23. Oxford: BAR International Series 500.

—— (1989b) 'Late Mesolithic settlements and cemeteries at Skateholm, southern Sweden', in C. Bonsall (ed) *The Mesolithic in Europe*, 367–78. Edinburgh: John Donald.

—— (1990) 'Dogs in fraction: symbols in action', in P. Vermeersch and P. van Peer (eds) *Contributions to the Mesolithic in Europe*, 153–60. Leuven: Leuven University Press.

—— (1993) 'The Skateholm project: late Mesolithic coastal settlement in southern Sweden', in P. Bogucki (ed.) *Case Studies in European Prehistory*, 31–62. London: CRC Press.

Last, J. (1998) 'Books of life: biography and memory in a Bronze Age barrow', *Oxford Journal of Archaeology* 17, 43–53.

Lévi-Strauss, C. (1964) *Totemism*. London: Merlin Press.

Lewis, G. (1980) *Day of Shining Red: An Essay in Understanding Ritual*. Cambridge: Cambridge University Press.

LiPuma, E. (1998) 'Modernity and forms of personhood in Melanesia', in M. Lambek and A. Strathern (eds) *Bodies and Persons: Comparative Views from Africa and Melanesia*, 53–79. Cambridge: Cambridge University Press.

Lopatin, I. (1960) *The Cult of the Dead Among the Natives of the Amur Basin*. The Hague: Mouton and Co.

Lucas, G. (1996) 'Of death and debt: a history of the body in Neolithic and Early Bronze Age Yorkshire', *Journal of European Archaeology* 4: 99–118.

Lukes, S. (1973) *Individualism*. Oxford: Blackwell.

McKinley, J. (1997) 'Bronze Age "barrows" and funerary rites and rituals of cremation', *Proceedings of the Prehistoric Society* 63: 129–45.

Marriott, M. (1976) 'Hindu transactions: diversity without dualism', in B. Kapferer (ed.) *Transaction and Meaning: Directions in the Anthropology of Exchange and Symbolic behaviour*, 109–37. Philadelphia, Pa.: Institute for the Study of Human Issues.

Maschio, T. (1994) *To Remember the Faces of the Dead: The Plenitude of Memory in Southeastern New Britain*. Madison: University of Wisconsin Press.

Mauss, M. (1990) *The Gift: The Form and Reason for Exchange in Archaic Societies* (trans. W. Halls). New York: Norton.

Meskell, L. (1996) 'The somatisation of archaeology: institutions, discourses, corporeality', *Norwegian Archaeological Review* 29: 1–16.

—— (1999) *Archaeologies of Social Life*. Oxford: Blackwell.

Miller, D. (1987) *Material Culture and Mass Consumption*. Oxford: Blackwell.

Mitford, N. (1998) *The American Way of Death Revisited*. New York: Alfred A. Knopf.

Mizoguchi, K. (1993) 'Time in the reproduction of mortuary practices', *World Archaeology* 25 (2): 223–35.

Montague, S. (1989) 'To eat for the dead: Kaduwagan mortuary events', in F. Damon and R. Wagner (eds) *Death Rituals and Life in the Societies of the Kula Ring*, 23–45. DeKalb: Northern Illinois University Press.

Moore, H. (1986) *Space, Text and Gender: An Anthropological Study of the Marakwet of Kenya*. Cambridge: Cambridge University Press.

—— (1994) *A Passion for Difference*. Cambridge: Polity Press.

Moore, J. and Scott, E. (eds) (1997) *Invisible People and Processes: Writing Gender into European Prehistory*. London: Leicester University Press.

Morris, B. (1991) *Western Conceptions of the Individual*. Oxford: Berg.

—— (1994) *Anthropology of the Self: The Individual in Cultural Perspective*. London: Pluto Press.

Mosko, M. (1992) 'Motherless sons: "divine kings" and "partible persons" in Melanesia and Polynesia', *Man* 27: 697–717.

—— (2000) 'Inalienable ethnography: keeping-while-giving and the Trobriand case', *Journal of the Royal Anthropological Institute* 6: 377–96.

Munn, N. (1986) *The Fame of Gawa: A Symbolic Study of Value Transformation in a Massim (Papua New Guinea) Society*. Durham, N.C.: Duke University Press.

Murray, D.W. (1993) 'What is the Western conception of the self? On forgetting David Hume', *Ethos* 21 (1): 3–23.

Nash, G. (1998) *Exchange, Status and Mobility: Mesolithic Portable Art of Southern Scandinavia*, Oxford: BAR International Series 710.

Nilsson, L. (1998) 'Dynamic cadavers: a field anthropological analysis of the Skateholm II burials', *Lund Archaeological Review* 4: 5–17.

Nilsson Stutz, L. (2003) 'A taphonomy of ritual practice, a 'field'-anthropological study of late Mesolithic burials', in L. Larsson, H. Kindgren, K. Knutsson, D. Leoffler and A. Åkerlund (eds) *Mesolithic on the Move*, 527–35. Oxford: Oxbow Books.

Oestigaard, T. (1999) 'Cremations as transformations: when the dual cultural hypothesis was cremated and carried away in urns', *European Journal of Archaeology* 2 (3): 345–64.

—— (2000) 'Sacrifices of raw, cooked and burnt humans', *Norwegian Archaeological Review* 33 (1): 41–58.

—— (in press) 'Kings and cremations: royal funerals and sacrifices in Nepal', in T. Insoll (ed.) *Archaeology and Religion*. Oxford: BAR.

Okely, J. (1979) 'An anthropological contribution to the history and archaeology of an ethnic group', in B. Burnham and J. Kingsbury (eds) *Space, Hierarchy and Society: Interdisciplinary Studies in Social Area Analysis*, 81–92. Oxford: BAR International Series 59.

Owoc, M.A. (2001) '"The times they are a changing": experiencing continuity and development in the Early Bronze Age funerary rituals of southwestern Britain', in J. Brück (ed.) *Bronze Age Landscapes: Tradition and Transformation*, 193–206. Oxford: Oxbow Books.

Palsson, G. (1996) 'Human–environmental relations: orientalism, paternalism and communalism', in P. Descola and G. Palsson (eds) *Nature and Society: Anthropological Perspectives*, 64–81. London: Routledge.

Parker Pearson, M. (1996) 'Food, fertility and front doors: houses in the first millennium BC', in T. Champion and J. Collis (eds) *The Iron Age in Britain and Ireland: Recent Trends*, 117–32. Sheffield: Sheffield University Press.

—— (1999a) *The Archaeology of Death and Burial*. College Station: Texas A&M Press.

—— (1999b) 'Food, sex and death: cosmologies in the British Iron Age with particular reference to East Yorkshire', *Cambridge Archaeological Journal* 9: 43–69.

Parker Pearson, M. and Ramilisonina (1998) 'Stonehenge for the ancestors: the stones pass on the message', *Antiquity* 72: 308–26.

Parry, J. (1982) 'Sacrificial death and the necrophagus ascetic', in M. Bloch and J. Parry (eds) *Death and the Regeneration of Life*, 74–110. Cambridge: Cambridge University Press.

—— (1994) *Death in Banaras*. Cambridge: Cambridge University Press.

Pentikäinen, J. (1984) 'The Sámi shaman: mediator between man and universe', in M. Hoppál (ed.) *Shamanism in Eurasia. Part 1*, 125–48. Göttingen: Edition Herodot.

Prine, E. (2000) 'Searching for third genders: towards a prehistory of domestic space in middle Missouri villages', in R. Schmidt and B. Voss (eds) *The Archaeology of Sexuality*, 197–219. London: Routledge.

REFERENCES

Rainbird, P. (2002) 'Marking the body, marking the land: body as history, land as history: tattooing and engraving in Oceania', in Y. Hamilakis, M. Pluciennik and S. Tarlow (eds) *Thinking Through the Body: Archaeologies of Corporeality*, 233–47. London: Kluwer/Academic Press.

Rasmussen, S. (1995) *Spirit Possession and Personhood Among the Kel Ewey Tuareg*, Cambridge: Cambridge University Press.

Rawcliffe, C. (1995) *Medicine and Society in Later Medieval England*. Stroud: Sutton.

Ray, K. and Thomas, J. (2003) 'In the kinship of cows: the social centrality of cattle in the earlier Neolithic of southern Britain', in M. Parker Pearson (ed.) *Food, Culture and Identity in the Neolithic and Early Bronze Age*, 45–51. Oxford: BAR International Series 1117.

Reay, M. (1959) *The Kuma: Freedom and Conformity in the New Guinea Highlands*. Melbourne: Melbourne University Press.

Renfrew, C. (1986) 'Varna and the emergence of wealth in prehistoric Europe', in A. Appadurai (ed.) *The Social Life of Things: Commodities in Cultural Perspective*, 141–68. Cambridge: Cambridge University Press.

Richards, C. (1988) 'Altered images: a re-examination of Neolithic mortuary practices', in J. Barrett and I. Kinnes (eds) *The Archaeology of Context in the Neolithic and Bronze Age: Recent Trends*, 42–56. Sheffield: University of Sheffield.

—— (1996) 'Henges and water: towards an elemental understanding of monumentality and landscape in late Neolithic Britain', *Journal of Material Culture* 1: 313–36.

Riches, D. (2000) 'The holistic person: or, the ideology of egalitarianism', *Journal of the Royal Anthropological Institute* 6: 668–85.

Robb, J. (2002) 'Time and biography: osteobiography of the Italian Neolithic lifespan', in Y. Hamilakis, M. Pluciennik and S. Tarlow (eds) *Thinking Through the Body: Archaeologies of Corporeality*, 153–71. London: Kluwer/Academic Press.

Rumsey, A. (2000) 'Agency, personhood and the "I" of discourse in the Pacific and beyond', *Journal of the Royal Anthropological Institute* 6: 101–15.

Russell, L. (in press) ' Resisting the production of dichotomies; gender race and class in the pre-colonial period', in E. Casella and C. Fowler (eds) *The Archaeology of Plural and Changing Identities: Beyond Identification*. New York: Kluwer/Plenum.

Sax, W. (2002) *Dancing the Self: Personhood and Performance in the Pandav Lila of Gharwal*. Oxford: Oxford University Press.

Saxe, A. (1970) 'Social dimensions of mortuary practices', Ph.D. thesis, University of Michigan.

Schmidt, R. (2000) 'Shamans and northern cosmology: the direct historical approach to Mesolithic sexuality', in R. Schmidt and B. Voss (eds) *Archaeologies of Sexuality*, 220–35. London: Routledge.

—— (in press) 'The contribution of gender to personal identity in the southern Scandinavian Mesolithic', in E. Casella and C. Fowler (eds) *The Archaeology of Plural and Changing Identities: Beyond Identification?* New York: Kluwer Academic/Plenum Press.

Shanks, M. and Tilley, C. (1982) 'Ideology, symbolic power and ritual communication: a reinterpretation of Neolithic mortuary practices', in I. Hodder (ed.) *Symbolic and Structural Archaeology*, 129–54. Cambridge: Cambridge University Press.

—— (1987a) *Reconstructing Archaeology: Theory and Practice*. London: Routledge.

—— (1987b) *Social Theory and Archaeology*. Polity Press: Cambridge.

Shennan, S. (1982) 'Ideology, change and the European Early Bronze Age', in I. Hodder (ed.) *Symbolic and Structural Archaeology*, 155–61. Cambridge: Cambridge University Press.

Shilling, C. (1993) *The Body and Social Theory*. London: Sage.

Sofaer Derevenski, J. (2000) 'Rings of life: the role of early metalwork in mediating the gendered life course', *World Archaeology* 31: 389–406.

Sørenson, M.-L. S. (2000) *Gender Archaeology*. Cambridge: Polity Press.

Spencer, H. (1857) 'Progess: its law and causes', *The Westminster Review* 67: 445–65.

Sperber, D. (1996) *Explaining Culture: A Naturalistic Approach*. Oxford: Blackwell.

Spiro, M. (1993) 'Is the Western conception of the self "peculiar" within the context of world cultures?', *Ethos* 21 (2): 107–53.

Strassburg, J. (2000) *Shamanic Shadows: One Hundred Generations of Undead Subversion in Mesolithic Scandinavia*. Stockholm: University of Stockholm Press.

Strathern, A. (1981) 'Death as exchange: two Melanesian cases', in S. Humphries and H. King (eds) *Mortality and Immortality: The Archaeology and Anthropology of Death*, 205–23. London: Academic Press.

—— (1982) 'Witchcraft, greed, cannibalism and death: some related themes for the New Guinea Highlands', in M. Bloch and J. Parry (eds) *Death and the Regeneration of Life*, 111–33. Cambridge: Cambridge University Press.

Strathern, M. (1988) *The Gender of the Gift: Problems with Women and Problems with Society in Melanesia.* Berkeley: University of California Press.

—— (1991a) 'Introduction', in M. Godelier and M. Strathern (eds) *Big Men and Great Men: Personifications of Power in Melanesia*, 1–4. Cambridge: Cambridge University Press.

—— (1991b) 'One man and many men', in M. Godelier and M. Strathern (eds) *Big Men and Great Men: Personifications of Power in Melanesia*, 197–214. Cambridge: Cambridge University Press.

—— (1992a) *After Nature: English Kinship in the Late Twentieth Century.* Cambridge: Cambridge University Press.

—— (1992b) *Reproducing the Future: Essays on Anthropology, Kinship and New Reproductive Technologies.* New York: Routledge.

—— (1996) 'Cutting the network', *Journal of the Royal Anthropological Institute* 2: 517–35.

—— (1998) 'Social relations and the idea of externality', in C. Renfrew and C. Scarre (eds) *Cognition and Material Culture: The Archaeology of Symbolic Storage*, 135–47. Cambridge: MacDonald Institute for Archaeological Research.

—— (1999) *Property, Substance and Effect: Anthropological Essays on Persons and Things.* London: Athlone.

Tainter, J. (1978) 'Mortuary practices and the study of prehistoric social systems', *Advances in Archaeological Method and Theory* 1: 105–37.

Tarlow, S. (2000) 'Comment', in C. Holtorf and H. Karlsson (eds) *Philosophy and Archaeological Practice. Perspectives for the 21st Century*, 123–6. Gothenburg: Bricoleur Press.

—— (2002) 'The aesthetic corpse in nineteenth-century Britain', in Y. Hamilakis, M. Pluciennik and S. Tarlow (eds) *Thinking Through the Body: Archaeologies of Corporeality*, 85–97. London: Kluwer/Academic Press.

Thomas, J. (1991) 'Reading the body: Beaker funerary practice in Britain', in P. Garwood, D. Jennings, R. Skeates and J. Toms (eds) *Sacred and Profane*, 33–42. Oxford: Oxford Committee for Archaeology Monograph 32.

—— (1996) *Time, Culture and Identity: An Interpretive Archaeology.* London: Routledge.

—— (1999a) *Understanding the Neolithic.* London: Routledge.

—— (1999b) 'An economy of substances in earlier Neolithic Britain', in J. Robb (ed.) *Material Symbols: Culture and Economy in Prehistory*, 70–89. Carbondale: Southern Illinois University Press.

—— (2000a) 'Death, identity and the body in Neolithic Britain', *Journal of the Royal Anthropological Institute* 6: 603–17.

—— (2000b) 'Reconfiguring the social, reconfiguring the material', in M. Schiffer (ed.) *Social Theory in Archaeology*, 143–55. Salt Lake City: University of Utah Press.

—— (2000c) 'The identity of place in Neolithic Britain: examples from south-west Scotland', in A. Ritchie (ed.) *Neolithic Orkney in its European Context*, 79–90. Cambridge: McDonald Institute.

—— (2002) 'Archaeology's humanism and the materiality of the body', in Y. Hamilakis, M. Pluciennik and S. Tarlow (eds) *Thinking Through the Body: Archaeologies of Corporeality*, 29–46. London: Kluwer/Academic.

—— (2004) *Archaeology and Modernity*. London: Routledge.

Thomas, P. (1999) 'No substance, no kinship? Procreation, performativity and Temanambondro parent–child relations', in P. Loizons and P. Heady (eds) *Conceiving Persons: Ethnographies of Procreation, Fertility and Growth*, 19–45. London: Athlone.

Tilley, C. (1989) 'Interpreting material culture', in I. Hodder (ed.) *The Meanings of Things*, 185–94. London: Unwin Hyman.

—— (ed.) (1990) *Reading Material Culture*. Oxford: Blackwell.

—— (1994) *A Phenomenology of Landscape*. Oxford: Berg.

—— (1996) *An Ethnography of the Neolithic: Early Neolithic Societies in Southern Scandinavia*. Cambridge: Cambridge University Press.

—— (1999) *Metaphor and Material Culture*. Oxford: Blackwell.

Turner, B. (ed.) (1984) *The Body and Society: Explorations in Social Theory*. London: Sage.

Turner, V. (1967) *The Forest of Symbols: Aspects of Ndembu Ritual*. Ithaca, N.Y.: Cornell University Press.

—— (1969) *The Ritual Process*. Chicago, Ill.: Aldine.

Van Gennep, A. (1960) *The Rites of Passage*. London: Routledge and Kegan Paul.

Vitebsky, P. (1993) *Dialogues with the Dead: The Discussion of Mortality Among the Sora of Eastern India*. Cambridge: Cambridge University Press.

Viveiros de Castro, E. (1996) 'Cosmological deixis and Amerindian perspectivism: a view from Amazonia', *Journal of the Royal Anthropological Institute* 4: 469–88.

Wagner, R. (1991) 'The fractal person', in M. Strathern and M. Godelier (eds) *Big Men and Great Men: Personifications of Power in Melanesia*, 159–73. Cambridge: Cambridge University Press.

Watson, J. (1982) 'Of flesh and bones: the management of death pollution in Cantonese society', in M. Bloch and J. Parry (eds) *Death and the Regeneration of Life*, 155–86. Cambridge: Cambridge University Press.

Weiner, A. (1992) *Inalienable Possessions: The Paradox of Keeping-While-Giving*. Berkeley: University of California Press.

Whitley, J. (2002) 'Too many ancestors', *Antiquity* 76: 119–26.

Whittle, A. (1997) *Sacred Mounds, Holy Rings: Silbury Hill and the West Kennet Palisade Enclosures*. Oxford: Oxbow.

Whittle, A., Pollard, J. and Grigson, C. (1998) *The Harmony of Symbols: The Windmill Hill Causewayed Enclosure*. Oxford: Oxbow Books.

Williams, H. (in press) 'Death warmed up: the agency of bodies and bones in early Anglo-Saxon cremation rites', *Journal of Material Culture*.

—— (2001) 'Lest we remember', *British Archaeology* 64: 20–3.

—— (ed.) (2003) *Archaeologies of Remembrance: Death and Memory in Past Societies*. London: Kluwer Academic/Plenum.

Williams, M. (2001) 'Shamanic interpretations: reconstructing a cosmology for the later prehistoric period of north-western Europe', Ph.D. thesis, University of Reading.

—— (2002) 'No nature, no culture, no difference. Swords in the later prehistory of north-western Europe', Paper presented at University of Manchester TAG 2002, session entitled 'Composing Nature'.

—— (2003) 'Tales from the dead: remembering the bog bodies of the Iron Age of north-western Europe', in H. Williams (ed.) *Archaeologies of Remembrance: Death and Memory in Past Societies*, 89–112. London: Kluwer Academic/Plenum.

Wolff, J. (1981) *The Social Production of Art*. New York: St Martin's Press.

Woodward, A. (2002) 'Beads and beakers: heirlooms and relics in the British Early Bronze Age', *Antiquity* 76: 1040–7.

Yates, T. (1993) 'Frameworks for an archaeology of the body', in C. Tilley (ed.) *Interpretative Archaeology*, 31–72. Oxford: Berg.

Yates, T. and Nordbladh, J. (1990) 'This perfect body, this virgin text', in I. Bapty and T. Yates (eds) *Archaeology after Structuralism*, 222–37. London: Routledge.

Zvelebil, M. (1997) 'Hunter-gatherer ritual landscapes: spatial organisation, social structure and ideology among hunter-gatherers of Northern Europe and Western Siberia', *Analecta Praehistorica Leidensia* 29: 33–50.

—— (2003) 'Enculturation of Mesolithic landscapes', in L. Larsson, H. Kindgren, K. Knutsson, D. Loeffler and A. Åkerlund (eds) *Mesolithic on the Move*, 65–73. Oxford: Oxbow Books.

INDEX